ANNOUNCING
THE REIGN OF
GOD

MORTIMER ARIAS

Evangelization
and the Subversive
Memory of Jesus

ANNOUNCING
THE REIGN OF
GOD

Wipf & Stock
PUBLISHERS
Eugene, Oregon

Wipf and Stock Publishers
199 West 8th Avenue, Suite 3
Eugene, Oregon 97401

Announcing the Reign of God
By Arias, Mortimer
Copyright©1984 Fortress Press
ISBN: 1-57910-563-7
Publication date 1/22/2001
Previously published by Fortress Press, 1984

To "the many"
and "the least of these."

The first outline of this book took shape while I was incommunicado in a military ambulance in my adoptive country in Latin America, while waiting long hours for what my captors and interrogators were going to decide about my future. I dedicate these pages to the many unheralded witnesses of Christ, the true martyrs who put their lives on the line for their Lord and their people, to denounce anything that opposes God's purpose for humanity, and to announce and incarnate the reign of God in our troubled world.   M.A.

Contents

Acknowledgments

I want to express my appreciation to my colleagues Cornish Rogers and William E. Pannell for reading the manuscript and encouraging its publication. I especially want to thank that brave apostle of the laity on both sides of the Atlantic, Mark Gibbs, who recommended my manuscript to the editors at Fortress Press.

The substance of this book was tried out for the first time in a course on "Evangelization in the Kingdom Perspective" at the School of Theology at Claremont, California, in Fall 1981, during a "golden exile" in that great theological institution. To the students who shared in this initial exploration; to the president of the school, Dr. Richard W. Cain; to the dean, Joseph C. Hough, Jr.; to the members of the faculty and other personnel of the school; to all who made it possible for us to stay there during a period of transition in our lives and who surrounded us with the most supportive community, we offer our deepest gratitude.

A particular word of thanks is directed to Stephanie Peterson, Barbara Hofrichter, and Ginny Vulgamore, who went through the accidented process of this manuscript, trying to type clearly my rather peculiar English writing. And, of course, to my wife Esther, who has lived vicariously the whole process of gestation of this book since the days of my prison experience, through our exile, and during the long moonlighting hours of its writing, I owe an unpayable debt.   Mortimer Arias

Introduction

Another book on evangelization? Yes, and without apology.

Evangelization is the announcement of good news. Good news is to be shared. This is what the gospel is all about. Anything that can help us understand, receive, and share the good news of Jesus Christ—the good news of the kingdom—is necessary, is good, and should be welcome. Anyone who has something to share—an insight, experience, vision, or conviction—should share it. For evangelization, in one way or another, is the task of the whole church and of every Christian.

This is not the final book on evangelization; it is not the last word. Rather, this book represents part of an ongoing quest that is occurring in the church throughout the world today. At the same time, it also represents the witness of a long personal quest that began forty years ago when I made, at age eighteen, the most eventful decision of my life—when I accepted Christ as my Savior and Lord and the gospel became the reason of existence for the rest of my life.

Evangelization is a generational task: "to incarnate the gospel in time." Every generation—inside or outside the church—has to be evangelized, that is, confronted with the good news of the kingdom in Jesus Christ. And every generation of Christians has the unique and nontransferable responsibility of sharing the good news with its own generation. This is the real meaning of John R. Mott's well-known slogan, "the evangelization of the world in this generation."

Our generation has come to a critical point in evangelization. On the one hand, there is a tremendous activity and creativity related to evangelization. No other comparable period has seen the explosion of evangelistic events, conferences, congresses, documents, pro-

grams, and activities as has the last decade, which included the
Synod of Rome on "The Evangelization of the Modern World"
(1974), the Lausanne International Congress on World Evangelization (1974), and the Nairobi Assembly of the World Council of
Churches with its section on "Confessing Christ Today" (1975)—to
mention only three of the major events involving Roman Catholic,
evangelical, and ecumenical Christians. All churches and denominations are trying to catch up with the evangelization wave and
are, accordingly, devising plans, strategies, methodologies, and
goals. Truly transnational corporations are dedicated to promoting
their own style of evangelization around the world with all the
available means of the media, marketing techniques, and electronic
resources. One such organization is launching a campaign to raise
one billion dollars in support of an ambitious blueprint "to present
the gospel to every person on earth in this decade!" Thousands of
books are printed and circulated every year on evangelization; most
of these fall into the category of methodology, the "how-to" manuals
for Christians and churches.

Not all of this activity or activism, however, is a sign of health and
creativity. There are signs of crisis in evangelization today. For
instance, there is a crisis in *credibility* in relation to the old ster-
eotype of "evangelism," which periodically gets redressed and re-
cycled with the most sophisticated means and techniques. There is a
crisis in *motivation* for evangelization, swinging from the old drive to
"save souls from hell" to the appeal for psychological salvation
through "possibility thinking"; from the "church growth" approach
to the rigorous challenge of "radical discipleship"; from the apocalyptic anticipation of doomsday to the expectation of human liberation in history. Crisis is apparent, too, in the search for an adequate
definition of evangelization. I have worked through more than one
hundred recent definitions ranging from "narrow evangelism" to
"holistic evangelism," with a broad spectrum in between. A crisis is
occurring also in the area of *methods* and *means* of communication,
in which the limitations of some favorite methods of the recent past
have become manifest. At the same time, the dangers of contemporary media—with their distortion of the content of the gospel and
their depersonalizing and alienating effects upon a mass of hungry
electronic consumers—have also been revealed.

There is, however, a more creative edge in this critical process: the new commitments and experiments of Christians in their own contexts around the world; new adventures in recovering the full biblical gospel, in incarnating the good news in lives and communities, and in witnessing to the kingdom of God in the most dramatic situations in the midst of the people and before the powers. This is particularly true in my own context in Latin America today. So this is an exciting time to recover, to live, and to share the good news of the kingdom!

"The good news of the kingdom" is not the usual way we describe the gospel and evangelization. Here in, then, lies the problem—and the promise!

For several years I have been involved in a search for holistic evangelization that is authentically biblical and contemporary. This quest was behind the Latin American Methodist Consultation on "Evangelization and Revolution in Latin America" which I had the honor to organize in 1966.[1] In 1974, while studying the Aymara Indians in Cochabamba, Bolivia, I spent my nights formulating the "Bolivian Theses on Evangelization in Latin America Today." In that document I submitted that evangelization should be genuinely *biblical, evangelical, holistic, humanizing, conscientizing, liberating, contextual, engaged, incarnational,* and *conflictive!* These theses have been discussed at the level of the national church and at another Latin American Methodist Congress on Evangelization. They have also been translated into several languages and adopted or discussed at various levels of the churches as suggestive of what evangelization today should be like. They remained as sketchy propositions, with some biblical references, to be developed and explored.[2]

In December 1975, I was asked to address the Assembly of the World Council of Churches on the missionary and evangelistic subject, "That the World May Believe," and again I tried to develop the same concept of holistic evangelization, this time in the wider context of the ecumenical movement and the world church.[3]

These were intuitions, supported by some experience, needing historical perspective and theological foundation. I tried to fill this need while preparing the Fondren Lectures and working on a Doctor in Ministry program at Perkins School of Theology in

1976/77. A broader acquaintance with the literature of evangelization prepared me to work out a "Critique of Traditional Evangelism," but at the time I was not able to devise a theological frame-
work for a new formulation of evangelization. I felt strongly that what
was needed, more than anything else, was a new encounter with the
gospel in our generation and in our particular situation, leading to a
new formulation of the evangelistic task today—if possible without
being conditioned by the traditional "hang-ups." Actually, that fresh
encounter with the gospel is already taking place in the most unexpected ways and places!

But I did not know how to proceed theologically. There were
some clear guidelines from the Scriptures—the incarnational style
of communication, the contextualization of the Word of God, the
prophetic witness, the early church's holistic ministry, and so on.
But how do we integrate the parts into a whole picture of biblical
evangelization?

In 1978 the theme of the World Conference on Mission and
Evangelism, to be held in Melbourne, was announced as "Your
Kingdom Come." The purpose of the missionary and evangelistic
task of the church was to be derived from the experience and
reflection of the churches on Jesus' prayer, "Your Kingdom Come." I
was excited over the prospect that we might find in this theme the
biblical and theological frame of reference for a theology of evangelization and mission. I began updating my reading on the teachings of Jesus and the "reign of God" in contemporary scholarship,
while trying to put the message of the kingdom in a way relevant to
our congregations in the city of La Paz, Bolivia. Responding to a
friendly request from Mexico, I formulated my first musings on the
Melbourne theme from a Latin American perspective in a book
published by Casa Unida de Publicaciones under the title *Venga tu
Reino* ("Your Kingdom Come").[4]

In July 1979 the Commission on World Mission and Evangelism
of the World Council of Churches invited some regional secretaries,
some executives, and practitioners of evangelism from around the
world, to explore new models for evangelization today. Since we
were in the preparatory period for the Melbourne Conference, the
question of "kingdom evangelization" was already haunting us. With
Al Krass, Al Johnson, and other world leaders on evangelism, we

were asking ourselves: What would "kingdom evangelization" look like? We made efforts to answer this question, but we did not know how to approach the subject from this perspective. We had a feeling, a hunch, however, that this was the direction to follow.[5]

When I was almost on my way to Melbourne, I tried for the first time to put together what may be called "kingdom evangelization" in lectures to be delivered at meetings in the United States, New Guinea, and Costa Rica.[6] In the process of developing these lectures, I was struck by certain findings that still puzzle and allure me.

First finding: The gospel in the Gospels—Jesus' good news—is none other than "the good news of the kingdom." And Jesus himself was the first evangelist of the kingdom.

Second finding: The kingdom-of-God theme has practically disappeared from evangelistic preaching and has been ignored by traditional "evangelism." The evangelistic message has been centered in personal salvation, individual conversion, and incorporation into the church. The kingdom of God as a parameter or perspective or as content of the proclamation has been virtually absent.[7]

Third finding: The kingdom of God, announced by Jesus, is multidimensional and all-encompassing. It is both a present and a future reality. It has to do with each individual creature and with the whole of society. It was addressed initially to "the lost sheep of the house of Israel," but was destined for "the whole world" and to "the end of the earth." It embraces all dimensions of human life: physical, spiritual, personal and interpersonal, communal and societal, historical and eternal. And it encompasses all human relationships—with the neighbor, with nature, and with God. It implies a total offer and a total demand. Everything and everybody has to be in line with it: "Turn away from your sins and believe the Good News" (Mark 1:15, TEV) of the kingdom of God.

So any partial or reductionistic version of the kingdom to which we have become accustomed (the transcendental kingdom in heaven or the inner kingdom of religious experience or the cataclysmic kingdom of the apocalypticists or the political kingdom of a new social order or the ecclesiastical kingdom of church expansion) is only a part of the total gospel of Jesus Christ that we are called to share and to proclaim.

Fourth finding: Those interested in the kingdom-of-God theme were, in general, not interested in the evangelistic task of the church, and those interested in evangelization have not as yet been interested in the kingdom theme. Still, the two belong together!

Fifth finding: The term "kingdom" is an unfortunate one in today's world: it is seriously questioned by many because of its monarchical political connotations and its associations with patriarchal structures and language. It is a particularly sensitive expression for those who are challenging the implications of sexist language and trying to translate the Scriptures in a way that expresses their faith in nonsexist language. "Reign of God" has been suggested as a better alternative, and it is already in circulation. In my original language— Spanish—we use the word *reino,* which includes the meanings of kingdom, reign, and realm. Because I speak another language, I do not pretend to understand all of the nuances of the English language nor would I attempt to solve this sensitive issue. I would like, however, to share in this concern and to express my solidarity with those who feel discriminated against or oppressed by language. I accept the fact, however, that "kingdom of God" has become a technical term in theology and religious language and a symbol so intimately related to Jesus' message that we cannot avoid it. I hope that our study of the meaning Jesus gave to this special term will show precisely that the reign of God puts under judgment not only old monarchies and patriarchal values but any system that denies God's given freedom and dignity to any human being. I will use the term "reign of God" whenever I refer to the general concept myself. Otherwise, quoting from Scripture or from others or with reference to "the kingdom," I will use the traditional English translation for the Hebrew *malkuth shamayim* or the Greek *basileia.*

Sixth finding: Meanwhile, I began to see that every item that I had been claiming as essential to a truly biblical and contemporary evangelization was a natural component of evangelization in the perspective of the kingdom. Every piece seemed to fall into the right place.

We could, for instance, take the theses on evangelization of the Bolivian document and see that each one of them is a part of the kingdom perspective! Who can doubt that the reign of God is truly *biblical?* And no biblical theme is more *holistic*—inclusive or all-encompassing—than the reign of God! No message could be more *evangelical* than this—Jesus' evangel. This message is *prophetic* and *contextual* through and through, both in its biblical and in its contemporary meanings. The announcement of the reign of God cannot but be *engaged* and *conflictive,* having to do with the realities of history and God's confrontation of the powers of evil in the human arena. In addition, it is *incarnational,* since the kingdom was incarnated in Jesus Christ—his ministry, death, and resurrection. The good news of the kingdom is also *humanizing,* calling human beings to claim their real dignity and heritage in God's secret design. It is *conscientizing,* arousing human conscience to an awareness of its plight and of the roots of sin and injustice. And it is truly *liberating* in its witness to the liberating power of God, working through human hearts, peoples, and societies toward the final liberation of creation. The reign of God perspective includes all our postulated characteristics of true evangelization—and more!

Why did I not see it before? Kingdom evangelization may be the answer to our present crisis. The vision of the reign of God can be the motivating force which takes us beyond the paralyzing effect of our contradictory and worn out motivations. A comprehensive New Testament theology of the kingdom can help us get beyond our present reductionisms and minitheologies of "evangelism." The multidimensional nature of the kingdom will not let us take refuge in our favorite dichotomies that plague our internal debate concerning the "spiritual and material," the "individual and social," the "historical and eternal," "evangelism and social action," and so on. Participation in the dynamic kingdom of God, which is in-breaking through history to its final consummation, may become the most creative experience to inspire new methods and means of sharing and incarnating the good news of the kingdom in our generation. And finally, while we hold together in the perspective of the kingdom, we will be centered in the one who is the author and fulfiller of our faith, Jesus Christ, the incarnated presence of the kingdom and "the proclaimer of the kingdom." Kingdom evangelization, then, cannot but be *Christ-centered evangelization.*

Seventh finding: This finding amounted to a humiliating and liberating realization, that is, that my "findings" had nothing original about them after all! The concern for the recovery of a kingdom perspective was already coming from every corner and in many ways. The Melbourne Conference certainly had a catalytic effect, but the conference theme itself was the manifestation of a process that had begun in the churches much earlier. This process has roots in the nearly century-long New Testament research on the historical Jesus and his original message.[8] It has antecedents in the full recovery of eschatology as a fundamental part of theology in its own right.[9] Missiologists had already begun to look at mission from the perspective of the kingdom.[10] Moreover, radical evangelicals, through biblical study and the critical analysis of the church and the dominant culture, are leading the way in the search for a more radical and inclusive concept of discipleship which will find its natural place on the horizon of the kingdom.[11] Some conservative evangelical scholars have also been working seriously for many years on this unfamiliar theme.[12] Evangelical strategists are finally discovering that the kingdom of God is the dominant theme in the Bible and that it should be claimed for mission today.[13] Meanwhile, in the Third World and notably in Latin America, the reign of God has been very much the basis for and a part of the vision of a new society, the renewal of the Roman Catholic church, and the phenomenal emergence of the basic-level Christian communities.[14] Its impact is especially evident in the recent constitution of the Latin American Council of Churches under the heading: "Engaged vocation with the kingdom."[15]

So, perhaps the time has come to recover in its fullness the biblical perspective of the kingdom for the mission of the church today and particularly for our evangelistic witness. We have tried many definitions of our own regarding mission or evangelism. Why not try Jesus' own definition of his mission—and ours? For Jesus, evangelization was no more and no less than *announcing the reign of God!*

How would evangelization look if viewed from the perspective of the kingdom? We will attempt to answer this question in the pages that follow.

ANNOUNCING
THE REIGN OF
GOD

1

The Good News of the Kingdom

> I must preach the good news of the kingdom of God . . . for I was
> sent for this purpose.   Luke 4:43

Jesus came announcing "the good news of the kingdom of God."
"That is my mission," he said (Luke 4:43b, Phillips). That was Jesus'
evangelization. But we have instead been preaching "the plan of
salvation" or some other evangelistic formula, and we have called
that "evangelism."

Herein lies our problem, our challenge, and our hope. We need
to measure our "evangelism" against Jesus' own evangelization. We
need to submit our evangelistic formulas and minitheologies to the
searching light of the whole apostolic proclamation and particularly
to Jesus' own proclamation.

"Evangelization" is a modern word that comes from "evangel,"
which means "good news." The words "evangelism" or "evangelization" do not exist in the New Testament.[1] But we have the noun
evangelion, which means "good news," "gospel," or "evangel" in
Greek. And we also have the verb *evangelizomai*, which means "to
announce good news." Both words were common in the Greco-
Roman world of the first century when the New Testament was
written. To evangelize was to bring good news about a great event
such as a victory in war, the coming of the emperor, or the announcement of the new age to come.[2] These were precisely the
words picked to describe the great event of Jesus coming into the
world to announce what God had done in him for humanity—the
gospel of Jesus Christ. And the books telling Jesus' story became
known in the second century as "gospels," while their authors were
known as "evangelists," that is, witnesses to and writers of the
evangel.[3]

1

JESUS THE EVANGELIZER

If we want to understand the real meaning of evangelization, we need to go back to the sources, to the evangel—to the gospel and to the Gospels. And, through these, we need to go back also to the one who was and is the gospel himself, the good news incarnated—Jesus the Christ.

Jesus Christ is both the evangel and the evangelizer. According to the witness of the New Testament, he is the center and content of the gospel, and he is the first evangelist of the kingdom.

This is one point about which there is solid agreement from the pope in Rome to the most recent evangelical strategists. In his elaborate apostolic exhortation on "Evangelization in the World Today," Paul VI said: "Jesus himself, the Good News of God, was the very first and greatest evangelizer."[4] Edward R. Dayton and David A. Fraser, research missiologists and graduates of Fuller Theological Seminary, make the same point: Jesus is the first evangelist of the New Testament. . . . Evangelism had its origin, pattern, and basis in the activity of the evangelist Jesus Christ. He is both, the evangelist par excellence and the one who embodied the Good News in dynamic works of power, signs, and authoritative teachings, which he gave to his disciples."[5]

If this is so, what was the nature or character of Jesus' evangelization?

JESUS' EVANGELIZATION

At the very start, we must recognize that Jesus' gospel is none other than the "good news of the kingdom of God." The first written gospel,[6] Mark, draws aside the curtain with a single pull when it declares: "The beginning of the gospel of Jesus Christ, the Son of God" (Mark 1:1). Without any other preamble and with a few more "pulls" (thirteen verses to be exact), the evangelist then sets the stage for his characterization of Jesus' evangelization: "Jesus came into Galilee, preaching the gospel of God, and saying, 'The time is fulfilled, and *the kingdom of God is at hand;* repent, and believe the good news'" (1:14–15). Thus Mark already names the gospel in two ways: "the gospel of Jesus Christ" (1:1) and "the gospel of God" (1:14). Now he is telling us what this gospel is all about: "the good news of the kingdom of God!"[7]

Luke, the physician, who wrote his Gospel for readers other than those addressed by Mark's Gospel and who had access to other sources concerning Jesus' ministry (Luke 1:1-4), tells us that Jesus defined his own mission in these terms: "I must preach *the good news of the kingdom of God* to the other cities also; for I was sent for this purpose" (4:43). To preach the good news was Jesus' purpose, Jesus' mission. This is why he came into the world—to announce the kingdom of God. This was his gospel.

Matthew's account, which was written at other times and locations, summarizes what is the consistent witness of the first three Gospels[8] (known as "synoptic" Gospels by the scholars because of their common content and shape): "Jesus went about all the cities and villages, teaching in their synagogues and preaching *the gospel of the kingdom,* and healing every disease and every infirmity" (Matt. 9:35).

Jesus' evangelization, then, was *kingdom evangelization.*

A fascinating feature of Matthew's summary of Jesus' ministry is not only that it confirms that Jesus' evangelization was centered in "the good news of the kingdom," but that it describes Jesus' holistic method: teaching, preaching, and healing. The good news of the kingdom is for the whole person—physically (healing), intellectually (teaching), and spiritually (preaching). But this distinction among the physical, intellectual, and spiritual does not do justice either to the biblical understanding of the human person as a total unity or to the inclusive character of Jesus' gospel. Certainly Jesus' evangelization was not limited to "saving souls" or to what we anachronistically might call "social services." Our usual discussions about "evangelism or social action" or "evangelism and social action" have nothing to do with kingdom evangelization.[9] Jesus points to a holistic ministry of good news as the sign of his divine mission. In response to John the Baptist's question, "Are you the one who is to come, or are we to expect some other?" (Luke 7:20, NEB), Jesus said to John's disciples: "Go and tell John what you have seen and heard: the blind receive their sight, the lame walk, lepers are cleansed, and the deaf hear, the dead are raised up, the poor have good news preached to them. And blessed is he who takes no offense at me" (Luke 7:18-23; see also Matt. 11:5-6).

Interestingly, Jesus' answer reminds us that the gospel of the kingdom is not only to be heard but to be seen. Where did we ever get the idea that there is a problem between word and deed in evangelization?[10]

Jesus' evangelization was also *holistic evangelization*.

In his inaugural message at the synagogue in Nazareth, Jesus applies to himself the messianic promises of Isa. 61:1–2; 58:6; and announces that the liberation promise of the Jubilee is now incarnated in his own ministry: "The Spirit of the Lord is upon me, because he has anointed me to preach good news to the poor. He has sent me to proclaim release to the captives and recovering of sight to the blind, to set at liberty those who are oppressed, to proclaim the acceptable year of the Lord" (Luke 4:18–19).

The Jubilee proclamation, reflected in the quotation selected by Jesus, pointed to the need for restitution of the means of life— including access to the land and the cancellation of debts—and demanded the emancipation of the slaves. The Jubilee proclamation of the prophets and the Jubilee legislation of several strata of the law, as well as the Jubilee celebrations of the liturgy and the Psalms imply that personal and social sins lead to accumulation of wealth, on the one hand, and to the deprivation of our fellow human beings, on the other. Personal and social sins lead to oppression of one group in society by other groups, and to the building up of injustices through attitudes and through social and economic structures which demand periodic restructuring and change. Both the prophetic proclamation and the prophetically inspired legislation were trying to recapture the liberating meaning of the Exodus and of the covenant, with its interaction of God's justice *(tsedeq)* and human and social justice *(mishpat)*.

This is precisely the promise used by Jesus to characterize his proclamation of the kingdom.[11]

Jesus' evangelization, then, is *liberating evangelization*—Jubilee evangelization!

APOSTLES' EVANGELIZATION

This was the kind of evangelization to which Jesus called his disciples. Mark tells how Jesus selected the twelve apostles from among his followers. "And he went up on the mountain, and called to him those whom he desired; and they came to him. And he appointed twelve, to be with him, and to be sent out to preach and have authority to cast out demons" (Mark 3:13–15).

They were called first to be disciples, "to be with him" ("to be his companions," Phillips), and then apostles ("sent out to preach").[12] After giving the names of the twelve apostles, Matthew repeats the commission which they received from Jesus: "And preach as you go, saying, 'The kingdom of heaven is at hand.' Heal the sick, raise the dead, cleanse lepers, cast out demons. You received without paying, give without pay" (Matt. 10:7–8).

In other words, the apostles' evangelization was to be a holistic proclamation, in word and deed, of the reign of God, just as Jesus' evangelization was. Actually, this commission looks very much like a preview in its universal form of the Great Commission for the apostles and future generations of Christians!

Luke gives us another insight: not only were the twelve apostles enrolled, but also the Galilean women became participants in the first and most amazing evangelistic team ever assembled in the history of Christian mission:

> Soon afterward he went on through cities and villages, preaching and bringing the good news of the kingdom of God. And the twelve were with him, and also some women who had been healed of evil spirits and infirmities: Mary, called Magdalene, from whom seven demons had gone out, and Joanna, the wife of Chuza, Herod's steward, and Susanna, and many others, who provided for them out of their means. (Luke 8:1–3)

This vignette is a revealing glimpse of what Jesus' evangelization was all about and how it was carried out. First, the gospel was "the good news of the kingdom of God." Second, it is suggested that it was not reduced to verbal proclamation: "preaching and bringing the good news" was done by a small community which was in itself a manifestation of the kingdom. There they were: the first fruits, the living signs of the coming kingdom, the transformed persons who made up the itinerant band of evangelists.

They were a show window, exhibit A of the kingdom. Look at them; what a strange mixture of people! They did not constitute a "homogeneous unit" of a rabbi and his itinerant male students— women were included! That must have been an unusual and even shocking thing to see. Nor did it look like a homogeneous women's

society either! There was Mary, famous in Magdala and beyond, not
precisely because of her social status, moral example, or philan-
thropic deeds—the one who had once been possessed by seven
demons (and it is left to the imagination to fill in the kind of
"demons" that dominated that poor woman). On the other hand,
there was another notorious woman of high social and official stand-
ing, the wife of King Herod's minister of economy (or budget
director), Chuza. One wonders how she came to Jesus and how the
royal minister felt about his runaway wife going around with this
itinerant preacher and his band of disciples, using their financial
resources to support the emerging movement! Susanna is another
outstanding woman, still remembered half a century later when
Luke was assembling materials for his Gospel. "And many others,"
the story says. They were as heterogeneous as they could be: men
and women, clergy and laity, fishermen, tax collectors, matrons,
former prostitutes, the affluent and the poor. But they had one thing
in common: they had been "cured," "healed," or "set free" by Jesus'
kingdom evangelization. They were living manifestations of the new
life in the coming kingdom, not only as individuals but also as an
integrated group in their life and witness: a base community committed to Jesus and his kingdom—an incarnational sign of the
kingdom.

Jesus' evangelization was also *incarnational evangelization.*

DISCIPLES' EVANGELIZATION

Jesus invited and sent others as participants in kingdom evangelization. He appointed a task force or lay witness team of disciples
known as the Seventy (some manuscripts read "seventy-two," which
would be a multiple of twelve, a body six times the size of the
Twelve), for a short-term mission: "After this the Lord appointed
seventy others, and sent them on ahead of him, two by two, into
every town and place where he himself was about to come" (Luke
10:1).

What were they going to do? The instructions were similar to the
ones given to the Twelve in Matthew 10. They were not to carry bag
or money; they would depend on hospitality. They were not supposed to spend the whole day on the road or tarrying in homes or
towns indefinitely. What was their message? Once again, it was the

reign of God! Tell the people, Jesus said, that *the kingdom of God has come near to you*" (Luke 10:9).

It was anticipated that the Seventy would not be welcomed everywhere; they were going out "as lambs in the midst of wolves" (Luke 10:3). But even if they are rejected, they must witness to the coming kingdom: "Even the dust of your town that clings to our feet, we wipe off against you; nevertheless know this, that *the kingdom of God has come near*" (Luke 10:11).

Their mission is one of peace, a sign of God's shalom, and it should be conveyed from the very first approach to peoples and homes: "Whatever house you enter, first say, 'Peace be to this house'" (Luke 10:5).[13] If there is openness, there will be communication and communion. If not, no pressure is to be exerted: "If a son of peace is there, your peace shall rest upon him; but if not, it shall return to you" (Luke 10:5–6). It is a mission of preparation for the coming of the one who incarnates the kingdom: He "sent them on ahead of him, two by two, into every town and place where he himself was about to come" (Luke 10:1). It is also a hopeful mission, in spite of the realistic warnings about a world of wolves and snakes: "The harvest is plentiful, but the laborers are few" (Luke 10:2).

The same call and the same challenge are to be made to any would-be disciple, as can be seen at a later stage of Jesus' ministry on his way to Jerusalem:

> As they were going along the road, a man said to him, "I will follow you wherever you go." And Jesus said to him, "Foxes have holes, and the birds of the air have nests; but the Son of man has nowhere to lay his head." To another he said, "Follow me." But he said, "Lord, let me first go and bury my father." But he said to him, "Leave the dead to bury their own dead; but as for you, *go and proclaim the kingdom of God.*" Another said, "I will follow you, Lord; but let me first say farewell to those at my home." Jesus said to him, "No one who puts his hand to the plow and looks back is fit *for the kingdom of God.*" (Luke 9:57–62)

Here again we have the Great Commission anticipated during Jesus' ministry: "Go and proclaim the kingdom of God!" And here we also have the meaning of discipleship: to follow Jesus without looking back, to follow the Son of man without any external guarantee, is the only way to be "fit for the kingdom of God." Evangelization and discipleship go together in the kingdom of God perspective. Kingdom evangelization and kingdom discipleship constitute the charter of the first three Gospels.

Jesus' evangelization was *discipleship evangelization*.

ONE GOSPEL

According to Matthew's version of the apocalyptic sayings, Jesus' intention was none other than to project this kingdom evangelization toward the future, beyond his passion and resurrection to the final consummation of the kingdom: "And this gospel of the kingdom will be preached throughout the whole world, as a testimony to all nations; and then the end will come" (Matt. 24:14).

There is only one gospel, the one that Jesus preached, the one that is going to be announced to the end of time: "this gospel of the kingdom." These prophetic words of Jesus amount to another pre-Easter version of the so-called Great Commission, the final command of the resurrected Lord (Matt. 28:18–20). If we are then going to appeal to the Great Commission as the foundation of the evangelistic responsibility for the Christian church, how can we do it without any reference to "the gospel of the kingdom of God"? Both in Jesus' proclamation and in the conscience of the church that preserved and transmitted it to future generations, there was only one gospel: the gospel of the kingdom!

It is impossible to read the first three Gospels with eyes open and not run up against the "reign of God" every few lines. The term "kingdom of God" in Mark and Luke and its equivalent in Matthew ("kingdom of heaven")[14] are repeated no less than one hundred twenty-two times—ninety times from Jesus' own lips!

Jesus' favorite method of teaching was through the use of parables. The parables indisputably belong to him. And what was their theme? The kingdom of God, of course![15]

The Lord's Prayer is also a kingdom prayer, which pivots on the central petition: "your kingdom come, your will be done."[16] And the Sermon on the Mount, which begins in the Beatitudes with the promise of the kingdom to the poor, is the Magna Charta of the kingdom![17]

How can we miss it?

Summarizing the results of a century of scholarship on the teaching of Jesus, Norman Perrin says:

The central aspect of the teaching of Jesus was that concerning the kingdom of God. Of this there can be no doubt and today no scholar does, in fact, doubt it. Jesus appeared as one who proclaimed the Kingdom; all else in his message and ministry serves a function in relation to that proclamation and derives its meaning from it. The challenge to discipleship, the ethical teaching, the disputes about oral tradition or ceremonial law, even the pronouncement of forgiveness of sins and the welcoming of the outcast in the name of God—all these are to be understood in context of the Kingdom proclamation or they are not to be understood at all. Of all the descriptive titles that have been applied to Jesus through the centuries, the one that sums up his historical appearance best is the one whose currency owes so much to Bultmann: Jesus is the Proclaimer of the Kingdom of God.[18]

The scholars are therefore of one mind regarding what the gospel of Jesus was all about. Why is it that we, the preachers and evangelists who are supposed to proclaim the gospel of Jesus the Christ, seem to have missed the central aspect of Jesus' teaching?

Even though many (including his own disciples) misunderstood what Jesus meant in his teaching on the reign of God, no one mistook the subject of Jesus' evangelization. To begin with, think of the Tempter himself! During the forty days when Jesus fasted and pondered in the desert about his future mission and its means, his mind perceived the pervasive influence of the Tempter in the specific suggestion to work through the political kingdoms of the times: "The devil took him to a very high mountain, and showed him *all the kingdoms* of the world and the glory of them; and he said to him, 'All these I will give you . . .'" (Matt. 4:8–9). Remember that this was real temptation for Jesus: the question of how to win the kingdoms of the world for the kingdom of God was very much in his mind!

The crowds perceived certain implications in Jesus' announcement of the kingdom of God and became the instrument of recurring temptations, intending "to carry him off and make him their king" (John 6:15, Phillips). Jesus' disciples, after hearing his kingdom evangelization for three years, took it so literally that they wanted to get on with it, disputing among themselves and demanding first place in Jesus' kingdom (Mark 10:37; Matt. 20:21). When the religious leaders, who had rejected and condemned Jesus on religious grounds, were looking for a plausible legal charge against him, it was easy for them to distort the meaning of what was

consistently Jesus' public theme: "We found this man subverting our
nation, opposing the payment of taxes to Caesar, and claiming to be
Messiah, *a king*" (Luke 23:2, NEB).

The emperor's representative, Pontius Pilate, was not certain what
"the kingdom" was all about, but he handed the Nazarene over to
the executioners and the crazy mob, saying, "Behold *your king!*"
Then he made the charge against Jesus official by placing over the
cross a caption, which he refused to change, saying, "What I have
written I have written" (John 19:22). The caption read: *"Jesus of
Nazareth, the King of the Jews"* (John 19:19). It was written in
Hebrew, Greek, and Latin, and it was read by many from the capital
city. The title is still there, for all to see and remember, in the
acronym over paintings of Christ dying on the cross: INRI. Jesus
died, accused of pretending to be a king. He died because he
announced the kingdom, and his enemies—in spite of all their
misunderstandings and distortions—realized very clearly some of
the implications of his kingdom evangelization!

The spectators at the crucifixion had their own theory about Jesus
and his kingdom, and they displayed it by laughter. With their
unconscious obstinacy, they made the crucifixion a cause of derision
and scorn, which became again a sort of prophecy and confession in
reverse: "He saved others; he cannot save himself. He is the *King of
Israel;* let him come down now from the cross, and we will believe in
him" (Matt. 27:42).

Jesus' companions were also aware that Jesus was concerned
about a kingdom. One of those who shared the execution on the
cross with Jesus joined the multitude in scoffing: "Are not you the
Messiah? Save yourself, and us" (Luke 23:39, NEB).

The other guerrilla who was condemned with Jesus took him
seriously in his good news of the reign of God. What he had heard
and seen helped him endure the ordeal of the crucifixion, and it
helped him to understand Jesus' life and his own life: "It's fair
enough for us . . . but this man never did anything wrong in his life"
(Luke 23:41, Phillips). As a revolutionary, he was able to see through
his human historical failure and perform his final act of faith and
hope beyond death in the kingdom announced by Jesus: "Jesus,
remember me *when you come into your kingdom*" (Luke 23:42). The
first evangelist of the kingdom, in his very last hour and in the last

hour of his damned fellow prisoner, opened the gates of the kingdom to his first convert and promoted him from this world to the
eternal reign: "I tell you truly, this very day you will be with me in
Paradise" (Luke 23:43, Phillips).

This is a strange first fruit of kingdom evangelization during the
time of Jesus' ministry on earth! Jesus, who had announced the good
news to the poor in *this life,* still had good news for the poor *beyond
this life,* when nothing could be expected from history. Jesus' evangelization, therefore, is truly holistic—for this world and for the
world to come!

From the beginning of his ministry in Galilee to the very end of
his life outside of the gates of Jerusalem, Jesus consistently announced the good news of the reign of God. That was his purpose;
that was his mission. Friends and foes were somehow aware of it.
How, then, can we miss it?

The most amazing witness concerning Jesus' evangelization is the
final one in the book of Acts—the only hint given in all of Scripture
about the meaning and content of the ministry of the resurrected
Lord. What was the content of Jesus' conversations with the emerging Christian community during the forty days of his Easter ap-
pearances? It would be fascinating to know what was going on
between the resurrected Lord and his disciples. Here is Luke's
summary of those eventful forty days:

> In the first book . . . I have dealt with all that Jesus began to do and
> teach, until the day when he was taken up, after he had given com-
> mandment through the Holy Spirit to the apostles whom he had
> chosen. To them he presented himself alive after his passion by many
> proofs, appearing to them during forty days, *and speaking of the
> kingdom of God.* (Acts 1:1–3)

The kingdom of God! This was also the pervasive interest of the
disciples of Jesus: "Lord, will you at this time restore the kingdom to
Israel?" (Acts 1:6). Once again, as throughout his earthly ministry,
the Lord was trying to move his disciples' minds from "the kingdom
[of] Israel" to "the kingdom of God."

This last vignette reveals that there was no esoteric teaching of the
living Lord to his apostles, but simply the ancient and unique theme
of the kingdom of God. It was more of the same. It was as if he were

ing to them, "this is what I have always told and shown you; go
and do the same. Go and announce the kingdom of God!"

AN ECLIPSE OF THE KINGDOM?

If this was Jesus' evangelization, kingdom evangelization, why
have we lost sight of it? It seems that we have, for a long time,
experienced an "eclipse" of the kingdom.

When we have an eclipse of the sun, it is because the moon is
between the sun and the earth—the moon's shadow is cast on the
earth. The eclipse may be total or partial, depending on whether the
observer can see a portion of the sun. But the sun is still there and,
as soon as the moon moves (or rather, when the earth moves in its
rotation and translation movements), the moon's shadow also moves.
In a short time, then, the sun can again be seen in all its splendor.

The message and perspective of the kingdom of God has always
been there in the biblical record, in the memory of the church, and
in the mission of the people of God. It has been a subversive
memory. What has happened in some periods has been the disap-
pearance of the language of the kingdom or the reduction of the
kingdom to a single dimension. However, like the sun which illumi-
nates the whole planetary system, including the earth (although not
directly seen within the shadow's cone), the kingdom of God has
been shining during the entire biblical witness and particularly in
Jesus' proclamation. It has been illuminating the apostolic mission
and expectation as well as the mission and expectations of the church
through the centuries.

We shall look first at the sunshine of Jesus' proclamation of the
kingdom before trying to understand and overcome the eclipse of
the kingdom in our evangelization.

2

The Presence of the Kingdom

If it is by the finger of God that I am expelling evil spirits, then the kingdom of God has swept over you unawares! Luke 11:20, Phillips

When we open the New Testament we find ourselves confronted by a mighty wind that is sweeping the land. Something radically new and dynamic is taking place in that small spot of the Middle East by the Sea of Galilee. Everything and everyone is turning around the moving center of this self-generated tornado.[1] The crowds are attracted to Jesus and drawn in by his amazing ministry of preaching, teaching, and healing. The sick are healed and those tormented by evil spirits are released and liberated. The first followers of Jesus left behind their jobs, boats, collecting offices, houses, and relatives and followed after him. The multitudes were amazed: "Never have we seen a thing like this!" The religious leaders felt disturbed and outraged, and from the very beginning they rejected the entire matter as evil: "This is the work of Beelzebub, the prince of the devils!"

Jesus, however, called it "the finger of God," the arrival of the kingdom of God.

Jesus' language in the Gospels is striking and unmistakable: "The time has come at last!" "The kingdom of God has arrived!" "Believe the good news!" (Mark 1:14–15, Phillips; Luke 11:20; Matt. 12:28); "Blessed are your eyes, for they see, and your ears, for they hear" (Matt. 13:16; Luke 10:23–24); "The kingdom of God is in the midst of you" (Luke 17:21); "This very day this scripture has been fulfilled, while you have been listening to it!" (Luke 4:21, Phillips).

This was the startling message of the first evangelist of the kingdom.

THE KINGDOM AS EXPERIENCE

The new element in Jesus' message of the kingdom was not only his unique use of the expression "kingdom of God" or "kingdom of heaven," but that this kingdom was near—was present. The idea of an eternal kingdom of God appears in the Hebrew tradition (Pss. 93:1; 97:1–6; 145:13), as does the affirmation of God's sovereignty over peoples, particularly over the people of Israel, and historical events.[2] But what Jesus proclaimed was that the kingdom of God is now present and operative in his own person and ministry!

Compare, for example, Jesus' own interpretation of his exorcisms with the accusation of his critics that he was acting under the power of the prince of evil spirits: "If it is by the finger of God [Spirit of God] that I cast out demons, then the kingdom of God *has come upon you*" (Luke 11:20; Matt. 12:28). Jesus not only affirms God's action in the healing of the possessed man, but he also proclaims that the kingdom is already present in this action. As Norman Perrin says: "The relating of the presence of the Kingdom to the present experience of a man is an emphasis unparalleled in Judaism. . . . This concentration on the individual and his experience is a striking feature of the teaching of Jesus."[3]

Or take Jesus' answer to those who were asking for signs to recognize the coming of the kingdom: "The kingdom of God is not coming with signs to be observed; nor will they say, 'Lo, here it is!' or 'There!' for behold, the kingdom of God is in the midst of you" (Luke 17:20).

The first part of Jesus' answer is negative: you should not look for external and cosmic signs of the coming of the kingdom, as in the apocalyptical expectations of the times. The second part of the answer is Jesus' bold proclamation that the kingdom is already present in his own ministry in their midst![4]

Meanwhile, the Gospel of Mark uses another striking expression in reporting Jesus' proclamation of the kingdom: "The time is fulfilled, the kingdom of God has *drawn near*" (other translations have: "is at hand" or "within reach").[5] The real meaning of this expression has been debated for decades, but it is difficult to deny that Jesus is announcing something that is happening, that is taking place in him and around him at this moment. To be sure, a response is demanded from the people to whom this announcement is given. But this is an announcement of something that God is doing right here and now. The kingdom is a fact, an event, a fulfillment.

Jesus uses the language of fulfillment to describe his own mission and ministry. After reading the messianic promises from Isa. 61:1–2 to his astonished fellow citizens in the synagogue of Nazareth, Jesus declared: "This very day this scripture has been fulfilled, while you have been listening to it!" (Luke 4:21, Phillips). God's intentions and promises in the Old Testament—the best hopes and visions of the prophets—are being fulfilled in Jesus Christ. He is the divine messenger (*mebasser*, the "messenger of joy" in Isaiah), the evangelist of the kingdom (Isa. 40:9–10; 52:7, 10; 41:27; 60:6). The kingdom is present in his words and in his deeds. The time of the good tidings has come.[6]

One of the most striking expressions on the coming of the kingdom is recorded in relation to Jesus' evaluation of John the Baptist's ministry and his own. While commending John as "a prophet, [and] much more than a prophet" (Matt. 11:9, TEV), indeed, "John the Baptist is greater than any man who has ever lived" (Matt. 11:11, TEV), "yet he who is least in the kingdom of God is greater than he" (Luke 7:28). Then Jesus goes on to draw the line between John's mission and his own: "The Law and the Prophets were in force until John's day. From then on the good news of the kingdom of God has been proclaimed" (Luke 16:16, Phillips). "For all the prophets and the law prophesied until John; and if you are willing to accept it, he is Elijah who is to come" (Matt. 11:13–14; Luke 7:24–28; 16:16).

Only a few miles separate the Jordan River, where John was baptizing, and the Sea of Galilee, around which Jesus' early ministry took place. Jesus and John thus belonged to the same place and time. Jesus was baptized by John, and John's disciples became the first disciples of Jesus. But between the two the threshold of the centuries has been crossed. John represented the end of one era— before the kingdom—and Jesus the beginning of another: the era of the kingdom, "the year of the Lord's favor." No wonder Mark put it so boldly: "the beginning of the good news." The kingdom has become a present reality!

C. H. Dodd was the first New Testament scholar in this century to insist on this definitive character of Jesus' ministry and proclamation. Based on the passages we have been quoting, which belong to the oldest and the best-probed works in the "Jesus tradition" before the Gospels were written, Dodd confidently affirms:

> These passages, the most explicit of their kind, are sufficient to show that in the earliest tradition Jesus was understood to have proclaimed that the Kingdom of God, the hope of many generations, had at last come. It is not merely imminent; it is here. . . . Whatever we make of them, the sayings which declare the Kingdom of God to have come are explicit and unequivocal. They are moreover the most characteristic and distinctive of the Gospel sayings on the subject. They have no parallel in Jewish teaching or prayers of the period. If therefore we are seeking the *differentia* of the teaching of Jesus upon the Kingdom of God, it is here that it must be found.[7]

Thirty years later Norman Perrin—after examining the different interpretations of the teachings of Jesus on the kingdom and applying the most severe criteria to determine what belonged to Jesus himself and not just to the Christian tradition of the early church—came to a similar conclusion:

> The hotly debated question as to whether this implies that the Kingdom is to be regarded as present, inbreaking, dawning, casting its shadows before it, or whatever, becomes academic when we realize that the claim of the saying is that certain events in the ministry of Jesus are nothing less than *an experience* of the kingdom of God.[8]

THE KINGDOM OF GRACE

The kingdom in Jesus' proclamation is a human experience, but it is not a human construction or a human program—it is God's gift of grace. Jesus himself incarnates the presence of this kingdom of grace.

The Gospel of Luke preserves a beautiful expression of Jesus: "Do not be afraid, little flock, for your Father is pleased to *give you the Kingdom*" (Luke 12:32, TEV). The kingdom cannot be earned or conquered, but only received as a gift. Consequently, do not be afraid, for it cannot be snatched from you.

Again and again Jesus insists that the kingdom is a gift of grace to be accepted without merit or pretension, freely and openly, as a child: "I assure you that unless you change and become like children, you will never enter the kingdom of heaven" (Matt. 18:3, TEV).

The good news belongs to the poor, to those who have nothing
and cannot assume or presume anything: "Blessed are you poor"
(Luke 6:20); "The Good News is preached to the poor" (Luke 7:22,
TEV; Matt. 11:5).

These are the signs of the presence of the kingdom, in the
ipsissima vox of Jesus.[9]

Jesus meant that the kingdom cannot be ensured by faithfully
observing rites and ceremonies in the Temple of Jerusalem, as the
priests and Sadducees claimed; it cannot be earned by strictly
obeying the law and its rabbinic interpretations, as the Pharisees
taught; it cannot be secured by fleeing from the world to a secluded
life of "purity" in the wilderness, as the Essenes attempted; it
cannot be conquered by the piercing swords of the violent rebellion
against Rome, as the Zealots pretended. The kingdom of God comes
as grace, and it has to be received as a gift. It can, however, be lost—
by presumption.

What is the kingdom of God, then? Jesus never defined it. But he
told many parables—his unique and inimitable way of teaching, his
way of revealing the utterly new and the unexpected from God.[10]

The kingdom of God is not, as the term "kingdom" might suggest,
the old order of a patriarchal despot, but the new order of love, the
kingdom of the Father. Jesus depicts God's motherly tenderness and
fatherly authority, and God's long-suffering parenthood, with the
unforgettable parables of the Lost Coin which the woman searches
diligently to find, the Lost Sheep that the good shepherd goes out to
find in the desert and bring back home with joy, the Lost Son, loved
by his father from the beginning, and received with generosity and
an extravagant display of joy and grace (Luke 15:4–32).

Human parents are not even the pale image of the Heavenly
Father—in whom we can really count: "Would any of you who are
fathers give your son a stone when he asks for bread? Or would you
give him a snake when he asks for a fish? As bad as you are, you
know how to give good things to your children. *How much more*,
then, your Father in heaven will give good things [the Holy Spirit]
to those who ask him!" (Matt. 7:9–11, TEV; Luke 11:11–13). Matthew's version says "good things," Luke's says "the Holy Spirit."
Actually, in Jesus' evangelization of grace, God is not only the giver

of "good things" and the "Holy Spirit" but the giver of everything
and all—the gift of the kingdom!

Jürgen Moltmann, in his last and intriguing book on *The Trinity
and the Kingdom,* presents this quality of the kingdom as the
kingdom of the Father:

> Jesus knows and proclaims the Lord of the coming Kingdom as his
> Father. This is where his unique authority is to be found. . . . The
> revelation of God's name as Father is Jesus' new and unique message.
> The name of Father stamps his proclamation of the coming Kingdom,
> his turning to the poor and sick, his prayers and his preparedness for
> suffering.[11]

Thus, what Jesus proclaims and teaches in his incomparable parables he shows also in his own life of prayer with the Father,[12] in his
dealings with his brothers and sisters in this world, and in his final
identity with the suffering Father on the cross.

Moltmann reminds us of the particular quality of the kingdom
with its relationships of freedom, love, and responsibility.

> Jesus did not proclaim the Kingdom of God *the Lord,* but the Kingdom
> of God *his Father.* It is not that Lordship is the mark of God's fa-
> therhood, but the very reverse: God's Fatherhood to Jesus the Son is
> the mark of the lordship and kingdom which Jesus preaches. That gives
> the kingdom he proclaims a new quality. The *basileia* only exists in the
> context of God's fatherhood. In this kingdom there are no servants;
> there are only God's free children. In this kingdom what is required is
> not obedience and submission; it is love and free participation.[13]

Is this not a particularly relevant understanding of the kingdom in
a world so full of religions, theologies, ideologies, and structures of
domination, rebellion, and manipulation? In a day when so many
peoples are struggling for justice and freedom from oppressive
societies; when so many young people are rebelling against author-
itarian religions; when others are running away from neglectful
parents; when women are seeking equality and liberation from the
exploitative use of patriarchal images of sexual subordination it is
essential to recover an understanding of God's fatherhood and the
liberating and fulfilling meaning of the reign of God that Jesus came
to inaugurate: the reign of fraternity, the true family of God, the
reign of grace.

HERE AND NOW

But Jesus did not announce this new order of the kingdom as a future hope or a reality distant from this world. He told and showed that this kingdom of grace is real and operative here and now.

The kingdom is present and active though it may work invisibly, like the Hidden Treasure that a man found in the field while working the soil; like the Mustard Seed that grows to become a big shrub; like the small portion of yeast in the dough, until it expands in the bread; like the New Wine inside the old wineskin until it bursts the skin; like the Seed in Good Soil, that grows and sprouts while the man sleeps without knowing how it grows. This is the "mystery," the secret of the kingdom of God (Mark 4; Matthew 13; Mark 2:22; and parallels)!

The presence of the kingdom is always a surprise, it comes unexpectedly, as a gift. It is a joyful discovery, like the Pearl of Great Price. Everything else is expendable, subordinate (Matt. 13:45–46; cf. *Gospel of Thomas* 76).

John Dominic Crossan, in his original interpretation of the parables of Jesus, considers the Hidden Treasure and the Pearl of Great Price (together with a lesser-known parable of the Great Fish in the noncanonical *Gospel of Thomas*) to be the key parables—the overture to and the paradigm for understanding all the others. They have a structural sequence (finds-sells-buys) that becomes the model for the experience of the kingdom of God as *advent, reversal, and action:*

> We are confronted, for example in the Treasure parable, with a man whose normalcy of past-present-future is rudely but happily shattered. The future he has presumably planned and projected for himself is totally invalidated by the *advent* of the Treasure which opens a new world and unforeseen possibilities. In the force of this advent he willingly *reverses* his entire past, quite rightly he sells "all that he has." And from this advent and this reversal he obtains the Treasure which now dictates his time and his history in the most literal and concrete sense of these words. It gives him a new world of life and *action* he did not have before and he could not have programmed for himself.[14]

How about this parable as a description of conversion? Crossan proposes that the three steps, advent-reversal-action, tell the story of Paul in his own geographical sequence: Damascus-Arabia-Jerusalem. Even the title, *Surprised by Joy*, of C. S. Lewis's story of his own conversion and Christian development, points to this same reality of the presence of the kingdom that comes as grace.[15] Jesus' parables, suggests Crossan, proclaim the kingdom of God in these three simultaneous modes of existence, some giving primacy to advent, some others pointing to reversal, and still others calling for action.

Jesus' parables are evangelistic through and through. Through parables Jesus announces the advent of the kingdom, displays the reversal of the new order upon the old, and invites to new life and action in the kingdom of the Father. The listener is left at the threshold to decide to enter into the new reality, to experiment with the new life, to embark on a new course—or else.

And Jesus concluded, "Listen, then, if you have ears!" (Mark 4:9, TEV).

THE FORGIVENESS OF SINS

But the presence of the kingdom is not limited to the incitements of the word. Jesus' listeners had the opportunity to experience the kingdom in the forgiveness of sins.

John the Baptist offered forgiveness of sins *after* repentance, confession, and restitution. Jesus announced forgiveness of sins *before* repentance, confession, and restitution (Matt. 3:1–8; Luke 3:3–18)![16] To the paralyzed man lowered through the roof of the house at Capernaum, Jesus said, "My son, your sins are forgiven" (Matt. 2:5, TEV). This man was brought to Jesus by his friends and probably had not said a word for himself. In confrontation with the teachers of the law, Jesus made this issue the deciding one regarding his authority and the meaning of his mission as the proclaimer of the kingdom of God: " 'I will prove to you, then, that the Son of Man has authority on earth to forgive sins.' So he said to the paralyzed man, 'I tell you, get up, pick up your mat, and go home!' " (Mark 2:10–11, TEV).

The forgiveness of sins was part of the eschatological hope. In Jesus' ministry it has become a fact—the kingdom has become experience. An experience of total healing: physical and spiritual—holistic healing.

The teaching of God's unconditional forgiveness and the need for this forgiveness mark the whole ministry of Jesus: the Parable of the Unforgiving Servant (Matt. 18:21–35), the Lord's Prayer on forgiving and being forgiven (Matt. 6:14–15), the Parable of the Pharisee and the Tax Collector (Luke 18:9–14). Forgiveness is the style of Jesus' public ministry in his dealing with notorious sinners like the tax collectors, the adulteress, and the prostitutes (Mark 2:17; Luke 7:50; 15:2; John 8:11). No wonder that forgiveness of sins becomes "the keys of the kingdom of God," entrusted to the church as its essential ministry (Matt. 16:19; 18:18; John 20:23).

This proclamation of free forgiveness, however, became a stumbling block for Jesus' contemporary religious leaders. Mark reveals the conflict and hostility against Jesus at the very beginning of his ministry among the people of Galilee (Mark 3:6). Hans Küng asks the question Jesus' critics were in fact asking: "According to this friend of tax collectors and sinners, is God, the holy God, supposed to *forgive sinners as such,* the unholy? But such a God would be a God of sinners: a God who loves sinners more than the righteous."[17] Exactly. This is the God of grace. The reign of God is here: grace in action.

But this forgiveness is not merely a judicial transaction or a stirring of religious feelings. The announcement of forgiveness in the reign of God is an act of total liberation. Since the "sinner" was an outcast in the religious community and in society, forgiveness was an act of inner liberation from guilt, fear, and inhibition, and an act of social liberation—of reconciliation and integration with the community (Luke 19:1–10). As Jon Sobrino says:

> Jesus' pardoning activity cannot be understood directly in terms of his own person. It too is a consequence of the approaching Kingdom of God. The forgiveness of sins exemplifies the same liberative activity that is embodied in Jesus' other signs. It is important to note that most of the accounts of Jesus' forgiving sins have to do with sinners who are not only alienated from God but also socially ostracized. Jesus seeks to liberate the sinners from their own egotism and sinfulness, but the social and religious backdrop is always one in which the sinners seem to have no possibilities left to them. His forgiveness is seen as the authentic liberation provided by God as opposed to the false liberation promoted by those who see sinners as people without hope or any possibilities at all.[18]

THE KINGDOM IS LIFE

The other amazing mark of Jesus' proclamation of the presence of the kingdom is that it is equated with life. To announce the kingdom is to restore life, to promise life, to celebrate life.

Look at Jesus' ministry to the poor. It is fundamentally a ministry of restoration of life, which typifies the "eschatological prophet" in the Old Testament (Isa. 26:19; 29:9–10, 18–19; 35:5–6, 8; 42:18; 43:8; 52:7; 61:1–3).

Take the message Jesus sent to John the Baptist in prison. In answer to John's question, "Are you the one who is to come, or are we to expect some other?" (Matt. 11:3, NEB), Jesus pointed to his healing ministry, while quoting from the promises and hopes of Isa. 35:5–6: "The blind recover their sight, the lame walk, the lepers are made clean, the deaf hear, the dead are raised to life, the poor are hearing the good news" (Matt. 11:5, NEB; Luke 7:22).

"There and then," emphasizes Luke's record, "he cured many sufferers from diseases, plagues, and evil spirits; and on many blind people he bestowed sight" (Luke 7:21, NEB).[19]

Küng has shown that the messianic promise selected and collated by Jesus was the opposite of the expectations of the pious monks of Qumran and the norms of their saintly community: "No madman, or lunatic, or simpleton or fool, nor blind man nor maiden, or lame or deaf man, and no minor, shall enter into the community, for the Angels of Holiness are with them."[20]

For Jesus, on the contrary, the disabled are precisely the natural candidates to enter into the kingdom of life! In his striking reversals, resorting many times to hyperbole, Jesus goes so far as to say that it is better to become disabled in order to enter into the kingdom, than to remain whole and be excluded. "It is better for you to *enter life* maimed than with two hands to go to hell. . . . It is better for you to *enter life* lame than with two feet to be thrown into hell. . . . It is better for you to *enter the kingdom of God* with one eye than with two eyes be thrown into hell" (Mark 9:44–47). What does this say about our late and reluctant recognition of the full humanity of disabled people within our societies?

And look how the kingdom is used as a synonym of life. To *enter into the kingdom* of God is to *enter into life*. Hell is the opposite of the kingdom of life. The opposition to life, the postponement of life values, in fact, is a rejection of the kingdom. This is why Jesus was so strong, passionate, even angry, when he came to the point of defending human life. When he was criticized by the Pharisees because his disciples were plucking and eating a few ears of grain on the Sabbath, Jesus answered in his own inimitable style:

> Have you not read what David did, when he was hungry, and those who were with him: how he entered the house of God and ate the bread of the Presence, which was not lawful for him to eat nor for those who were with him, but only for the priests? . . . If you had known what this means, "I desire mercy, and not sacrifice," you would not have condemned the guiltless. For the Son of man is lord of the sabbath. (Matt. 12:3–8)

In the face of human need and human life there is no other more sacred value, be it the law, the temple, the Sabbath, or whatever.

And when the Pharisees were watching to see if he would cure a man with a withered arm on the Sabbath, to bring a charge against him, Jesus put the question to them bluntly, "Is it lawful on the sabbath to do good or to do harm, to save life or to kill?" (Mark 3:4).[21] Jesus did not wait for their agreement or answer. Instead he performed one more act of proclamation of the kingdom of life: "Then he said to the man, 'Stretch out your hand.' And the man stretched it out, and it was restored, whole like the other" (Matt. 12:13).

The forces of antilife were not happy at all: "The Pharisees went out and took counsel against him, how to destroy him" (Matt. 12:14).

The kingdom of life has come in Jesus Christ—affirming human life (physical, psychological, spiritual, social, eternal), defending human life, restoring human life, and celebrating human life. This is the implication of Jesus' response to those who criticized him and his disciples for not fasting: "Do you expect the guests at a wedding party to go without food? Of course not!" (Mark 2:18–22, TEV; Matt. 9:14–17; Luke 5:33–39; cf. John 2:1–11).

To enter into the kingdom is to enter into life, full life, abundant life, eternal life—here and hereafter, now and forever. This was Jesus' holistic evangelization.

THE OPEN TABLE

The announcement of the kingdom in Jesus came not only as a restoration of life and of relationships with God through forgiveness of sins, but also as a restoration of community.

Jesus intrigued his hearers with his reversal parables and sayings. The most dramatic parable of Jesus' evangelization is his acted parable of the open table with sinners. It did not merely intrigue, but attracted the most notorious sinners and, at the same time, repelled and infuriated the most notorious righteous people.

It is amazing how many times in the Gospels we find Jesus participating in a meal. This was such a feature in Jesus' ministry that he was considered by some to be a "glutton" and a "drinker." He accepted all kinds of invitations, from poor and rich people, from publicans and Pharisees. He was the host in his borrowed house and sometimes even invited himself to dinner (Mark 2:15; Luke 7:36; 11:37; 14:1; 15:2; 19:5). Those meals were occasions for joy and fellowship, and some people believe that many of Jesus' parables began as stories told at table.[22] But the meals were not merely social events—they were signs of the presence and the hope of the king-dom, an anticipation of the messianic banquet. What made Jesus' meals such centers of controversy and fury was that he ate and drank with public sinners. This could not be something from God. People expected the Messiah to leave out the sinners and the evil-doers!

For the public sinners, the publicans and harlots, the social and religious marginal people, however, the open table became good news—the good news of the kingdom of grace. The act of eating and drinking was an act of proclamation! And it became the occasion for the proclamation by word: " 'Why does he eat with such people?' Jesus heard them and answered, 'People who are well do not need a doctor, but only those who are sick. I have not come to call respect-able people, but outcasts' " (Mark 2:16–17, TEV; Matt. 9:11–13; Luke 5:30–32).

Sobrino perceives the liberating quality of this evangelization of the arrival of the kingdom in Jesus' ministry:

> Both his miracles and his forgiveness of sins are primarily signs of the arrival of the kingdom of God. They are signs of liberation. . . . Jesus proclaims that the arrival of the kingdom is salvation and that the kingdom was the decisive connotation of liberation. But this salvation and liberation is not expressed solely in words (sermons and parables); it is also expressed in *deeds*. The need to preach the good news in deeds flows of necessity from the reality of God as described above. . . . Jesus' *actions* are not simply accompaniments to his words. . . . They are meant to demonstrate the Kingdom of God.[23]

This proclamation of grace in action was precisely the one that would take Jesus to the cross. "Paradoxically," as Sobrino says, "it is this teaching of God's kingdom as grace that proves to be the major obstacle for accepting Jesus."[24]

This was true with Jesus and it will be true with us—if we are faithful evangelists.

Kingdom evangelization is holistic—and it is costly.

The Imminence of
the Kingdom

Be ready for action, with belts fastened and lamps alight. Be like
men who wait for their master's return.   Luke 12:35–36, NEB

There is an unbearable tension in Jesus' proclamation of the
kingdom. The kingdom has come—and will come. The time is
fulfilled—but we await the consummation. The kingdom is experience—but it is also hope. It is present and imminent. It is "already"
and "not yet."[1]

"The kingdom will come with power and glory." We are "in the
last days" but "nobody knows the hour or the day" of the end, "not
even the Son." The kingdom is dawning, but we are still in the hour
of darkness—in the midst of sin, suffering, and death—looking forth
to the full day. The kingdom is here, hidden, at work, but only as
seed, sprout, and first fruits; it is not yet the time of the harvest. And
yet everything points to that end—to the consummation of the
kingdom. Jesus came to announce an eschatological kingdom![2]

Meanwhile, we are like people who wait—the people of hope.
And we are invited to be signs of the coming kingdom, to "seek first
the kingdom of God," and to pray saying, "your kingdom come, your
will be done on earth as it is in heaven." This was Jesus' announcement of the imminent kingdom—the mobilizing promise to the
people of God in the midst of history.[3]

Jesus announced the coming reign of God many times and in
many ways: in his teachings to his disciples, in his public preaching,
in personal conversations with seekers, before the authorities or his
enemies, in parables, in actions, in solemn utterances dressed in
apocalyptic imagery, and in the most intimate moments of prayer.[4]
Rudolph Bultmann, the scholar and theologian who has been influ-

ential in translating the message of the kingdom into existentialist·
categories (as a present reality, as the immediacy of God in our
present personal experience), had to accept that in the New Testament record Jesus proclaimed a future kingdom.

> The Kingdom of God is genuinely future. . . . There can be no doubt
> that according to Jesus' thought the Kingdom is the marvelous, new,
> wholly other, the opposite of anything present. . . . Thus, if we wish to
> understand the message of Jesus, it is not possible to ignore the future
> character of the Kingdom of God, nor to minimize the distance of God
> in the present.[5]

PARABLES ON THE FUTURE AND OF CONTRAST

Let us consider Jesus' parables on the future. Even those parables
which stress the *presence* of the kingdom also point to a *future*
consummation of the kingdom.

For instance, in the Parable of the Sower the seed of the kingdom
is already sown but the *harvest* will be in the future, despite the
apparent failure of the seed that fell in bad soil (Mark 4:3–8; Matt.
13:3–8; Luke 8:5–8). In the Bible, the harvest is the symbol of the
new age, a symbol of consummation (Isa. 9:3; Ps. 126:6; Joel 3:13;
Matt. 3:12; 9:37–38; Luke 3:17; 10:2; Gal. 6:7–9; Rev. 14:15, 18;
John 4:35–36).

The same is true in the parables of contrast, the parables of the
Mustard Seed and the Leaven in the Dough. The small portion of
leaven and the little seed represent the humble beginnings of the
kingdom in Jesus' ministry, destined to leaven the whole mass of the
world and to become a tree where the nations (the birds) will find a
shadow (Mark 4:30–32; Matt. 13:31–33; Luke 13:18–21).

God's reign is at work, secretly, like the seed sown by the Patient
Husbandman, who confidently awaits the harvest. While the kingdom is moving toward its consummation, evil in the world is active
and mixed with the seed and fruit of the kingdom, as told in the
parables of the Tares and the Wheat and the Fishnet. Good and evil
are mixed in this world until the final judgment. This is "the
mystery of the kingdom of God"—the already and the not yet (Mark
4:11, 26–29; Matt. 13:24–30, 36–43, 47–50).

PARABLES OF CRISIS AND PAROUSIA

There are five parables known as crisis or parousia parables, which
have a clear future component. Matthew uses the word parousia to

refer to Jesus' "appearance" or "presence" at the end of time (Matt. 24:27, 37, 39).[6]

First, we have the parable of the Nocturnal Burglar (Matt. 24:43–44; Luke 12:39–40). The Son of man will come at the end time without any previous notice, as a thief in the night. Therefore, be ready, because one does not know when he will come. A similar parable is that of the Doorkeeper who is left to keep the night watch, waiting for the sudden return of the lord of the house (Mark 13:33–37; Luke 12:35–38; Matt. 24:42).

With the warning to watch, there is a general call to a life style proper to people living in the expectation and hope of the coming kingdom: "Be ready for action, with belts fastened and lamps alight. Be like men who wait for their master's return from a wedding-party" (Luke 12:35–36, NEB).

The next parable, the Servant Entrusted with Supervision, stresses even further the responsibility of the steward in administering the household and in relating to other servants. The waiting is an active waiting (Matt. 24:45–51; Luke 12:41–46). This theme is further elaborated in the parable of the Talents, which contrasts good servants with bad servants in the way they fulfilled their responsibility, the way they worked with their talents, during the time of waiting (Matt. 25:14–30; Luke 19:12–27).

Finally, there is the parable of the Ten Maidens, based on Palestine's marriage customs in Jesus' time. The severe note of final loss for the five foolish maidens who had no oil and were excluded from the seven-days' wedding feast is balanced by the dominant theme of the wedding celebrations (Matt. 25:1–13).[7]

The wedding is an ancient symbol of God's relationship with his people in the Old Testament. Here, and throughout the whole ministry of Jesus, it becomes the symbol of the coming kingdom. God is preparing the future feast of salvation, the cosmic final wedding of God with his created and redeemed humanity (Isa. 25:6–9; Ps. 81:16; Jer. 31:31; Zech. 8:8, 19–23). This is what God has in store for our future because, as Alfred C. Krass has so beautifully put it, our God is a "feast-maker God," a "wedding-maker God"![8]

Another parable, in two versions, has a similar theme and the same proclamation of hope and consummation. In Matthew (22:1–14), it is the parable of the Wedding Feast that a king prepared for his son. The wedding theme, pointing to the messianic banquet, is

reinforced by a second parable, on the Wedding Garment, inter-
woven with the first one (vv. 11–13). In Luke (14:16–24), the parable
is about a Great Feast that a man gave in honor of his guests. The
kingdom theme is apparent throughout the story.[9]

During one of those dinners, when one of the guests, in a pious
mood, said, "Happy the man who shall sit at the feast in the kingdom of God!" (Luke 14:15, NEB), Jesus told the story of the "big
dinner party" which was missed by the originally invited guests.
The "feast-maker God" had displayed his royal invitation: "Please
come, everything is now ready!" (Luke 14:17, NEB). A feature
common to both parables is that the invited guests excused themselves because they were too busy. So the king (the rich man) sent
his servants all over the city to invite the marginal people—the
poor, the maimed, the blind, and the lame, "the bad and good," "as
many as you find." They should bring all kinds of people, "so that,"
the host said, "my house may be filled" (Luke 14:23). And "the
wedding hall was filled with guests" (Matt. 22:10).

FUTURE-ORIENTED CELEBRATIONS

The kingdom is imminent as an unforeseeable catastrophe. At the
same time, however, there is the promise of a future consummation
of joy and fulfillment—like the expectations underlying a wedding
feast and marriage. The great dinner with its universal guests is the
luminous and dominant backdrop of Jesus' proclamation of this
future consummation of the reign of God revealed throughout his
ministry. Jesus' meals during his ministry are the natural settings
(Sitz im Leben) of these unforgettable parables of the kingdom's final
banquet.[10] Jesus' table fellowship was in itself a proclamation of the
consummation of the kingdom, a sign, an anticipation of the coming
reign of God.

Jesus' last meal with his disciples—set by Jesus himself in the
context of the consummation—is another future-oriented celebration: "Believe me, I shall not eat the Passover again until all that it
means is fulfilled in the kingdom of God" (Luke 22:16, Phillips).

The early Christian community—from which Paul received the
sacred trust of the eucharistic tradition—understood quite well that
in breaking the bread and drinking the cup, they were not only
celebrating a memorial of Jesus' death but proclaiming, by antici-

pated celebration, the future consummation of the reign of God: "For as often as you eat this bread and drink the cup, you proclaim the Lord's death *until he comes*" (1 Cor. 11:26).

Following the intention of Jesus, the Eucharist became the central celebration of the pilgrim community of the kingdom and the ever-reenacted proclamation of the coming reign of God. After the cross and the resurrection, between Pentecost and the parousia, the church will be called to *celebrate* and to *proclaim* a kingdom that has already come, is coming now, and will come in its fullness at the end of time.

So through teaching and celebration, Jesus was announcing the kingdom as promise and fulfillment, as already and not yet.[11]

THE LORD'S PRAYER AND THE BEATITUDES

Two of the most characteristic pieces of Jesus' teaching—the Lord's Prayer and the Beatitudes—are both inserted in the present experience of the community of the kingdom in this world and projected to the final consummation of the kingdom in its fullness. Take the triple "thou petitions" of the Lord's Prayer: "Hallowed be thy name. Thy kingdom come. Thy will be done, on earth as it is in heaven" (Matt. 6:9-10; Luke 11:2).

As Krister Stendahl said in his studies on the Lord's Prayer at the Melbourne Conference on "Your Kingdom Come": "The three first prayers (your name—your kingdom—your will) are actually three ways of expressing the same urgent petition: the redemption of God's fallen and rebellious creation. . . . In praying for the coming of that kingdom we pray for a redeemed, a healed, amended creation."[12]

The Lord's Prayer is a prayer for every day until the kingdom comes, to be used in a manner similar to the obstinate importuning of the poor widow with the unjust judge (Luke 18:1-6). It is a future-oriented prayer as Ernst Lohmeyer has rightly insisted: "The whole of this prayer is hope and longing for the day of consummation . . . all is focused in the imminent future."[13]

The "already" and the "not yet" are right there—at the heart of the Lord's Prayer.

The modern translations of the Beatitudes, those precious gems of Jesus' teaching, also suggest the inherent tension between the presence of the kingdom *in the experience* of its members (the poor, the mourners, the meek, those who hunger and thirst for justice, the merciful, the pure in heart, the peacemakers, the persecuted for the sake of justice) *and the hope* of its consummation in the kingdom of heaven (with its final consolation, its vision of God, and its divine community) when the earth will be inherited and peace and justice shall reign forever. While the first and last Beatitudes are in the present tense ("blessed *are* the poor in spirit," "blessed *are* those who are persecuted"), the others stress the future *("shall* be comforted," *"shall* inherit the earth," *"shall* see God").[14]

FUTURIST SAYINGS OF JESUS

There are, however, other sayings of Jesus that point clearly to the future coming of the kingdom. Here is his striking picture of a universalistic kingdom, which reverses all the expectations of the pious and self-righteous religious leaders of his day:

> I assure you that many will come from the east and the west and sit down with Abraham, Isaac, and Jacob at the feast in the Kingdom of heaven. But those who should be in the Kingdom will be thrown out into the darkness. (Matt. 8:11–12, TEV)

> People will come from the east and the west, from the north and the south, and sit down at the feast in the Kingdom of God. (Luke 13:29, TEV)

"Entering into the kingdom" is also projected into the future as a promise and a warning:

> I tell you then, that your justice must be a far better thing than the justice of the scribes and Pharisees before you can *set foot* in the Kingdom of heaven at all! (Matt. 5:20, combined)

> Not everyone who calls me "Lord, Lord" *will enter* the Kingdom of heaven, but only those who do what my Father in heaven wants them to do. (Matt. 7:21, TEV; Mark 10:15, 23)[15]

Characteristic of Jesus' style are the reversal sayings, in which Jesus contrasts God's dealings with human expectations, world standards with the kingdom life style, and present realities of sin with the final new order of the kingdom:

> Everyone who makes himself [herself] great will be humbled, and

everyone who humbles himself [herself] will be made great. (Luke 14:11, TEV)

But many who now are first will be last, and many who now are last will be first. (Mark 10:31, TEV)

Happy are you who are hungry now; you will be filled! Happy are you who weep now; you will laugh! (Luke 6:21, TEV; Mark 10:31; cf. also Mark 8:35)

In his future-oriented utterances Jesus speaks freely of judgment—the present everyday judgment and the final judgment—of punishments and rewards; he also paints the glory of God's kingdom with bright colors, in terms of light, life, glory, salvation, and resurrection (Matt. 6:1–6; 10:40–42; 12:41–42; Luke 6:32–34; 11:31–32; 16:18; 19:1–10; Matt. 10:22; 25:21, 23; Mark 10:29–30, 37, 47; 9:43–47; Luke 20:27–40; Mark 12:18–27; Matt. 22:23–33).

For generations the most intriguing term for Jesus has been the only one he applied to himself: *"The Son of man."* No one called him that, but when his disciples acclaimed him as Messiah, he would answer instead: "The Son of man. . . ." It is a complex expression having several meanings in the Gospels and in the apocalyptic literature of the period immediately preceding Jesus' coming. Jesus used it in at least three different ways: (1) "Son of man" means simply "human" (Mark 2:27; Matt. 12:31–32; Luke 12:10); (2) "Son of man" applies to Jesus' earthly career, including his suffering and death (Mark 8:31; 9:2; 9:31; 10:33); (3) "Son of man" refers to the heavenly man (in the tradition of the book of Daniel) who will be associated with the parousia and the consummation of the kingdom "in power and glory" (Mark 8:38; 13:26; 14:62; Matt. 10:23; 24:27, 37; Luke 17:22, 24, 26).[16] Matthew makes explicit the relationship between the Son of man and the future consummation of the kingdom, "when the Son of man comes as King . . ." (Matt. 25:31–34). In the Parable of the Judgment of the Nations the Son of man and the King are one and the same! And again, in one of the most characteristic futuristic sayings of Jesus: "There are some here who will not die until they have seen the Son of Man come as King" (Matt. 16:28, TEV; cf. Mark 9:1).

Jesus was a poet and as such he combined many rich and suggestive images of his own with concepts and expressions from the prophetic, the rabbinic, and the apocalyptic traditions. The question, however, is, How are we to interpret those poetic figures, rabbinic references, prophetic utterances, apocalyptic images, and flashy words? What is the meaning for today of Jesus' proclamation of the future kingdom?

WAS JESUS AN APOCALYPTICIST?

For over a century apocalyptic preachers have taken literally some of the apocalyptic sections of the Gospels (but particularly also Revelation and Daniel), trying to fit these to current events—earthquakes, astronomical phenomena, wars, plagues, and the dreadful prospect of nuclear Armageddon. Can they claim Jesus on their side? Is their evangelization Jesus' kingdom evangelization?

Was Jesus an apocalypticist or a prophet? What is the difference and what is its importance for kingdom evangelization?[17]

Both prophets and apocalypticists proclaimed God's action in the future. The prophets gave shape to their eschatological hope in terms of God's coming judgment and salvation in history, calling people to love and justice in response to God's action. Apocalyptic writers, instead, projected a sort of deterministic future, warning of an impending and unavoidable action, such as a storm, which will bring the world to an end. Prophets appealed to human freedom and conscience, by calling to repentance and conversion and stressing God's promises and the openness of the future. The apocalyptic writers, on the contrary, threatened the total destruction of the world, the punishment of the enemies of the faithful people of God, and the salvation of the elect. For the apocalypticists everything was fixed, nothing could be changed.[18]

It is obvious that Jesus belonged to the prophetic eschatological tradition. He did not share the fatalistic ideology and the limited horizon of the pseudonymous apocalyptic writers. Jesus himself compared his mission and his fate to that of a prophet (Mark 6:4// Matt. 13:57//Luke 4:24; Luke 13:33), and he behaved like a prophet, demanding repentance (Luke 13:3, 5), and calling to change in the face of coming judgment (Mark 1:15). The people regarded Jesus as a prophet (Mark 6:15//8:28//Luke 9:7–9; Mark 14:65; Matt. 21:46), though Jesus himself plainly declared that he was "more than a prophet" (Matt. 12:41–42; 11:11–12; Luke 16:16).

There is, however, no doubt that Jesus used apocalyptic language as a painter uses colors and brushes. Jesus spoke of judgment of nations and generations; of the general resurrection and the "regeneration" of the world; of the "last day" and the "age to come"; of the "bosom of Abraham" and "Gehenna"; of the messianic feast and the outer darkness; of the falling of Satan from heaven and the coming of the Son of man with his angels for the final harvest, and so on.[19]

And yet while Jesus spoke of the sudden and decisive end of the world, he did not fall into the apocalyptic trap of giving symbolic numbers and fixing the times and seasons of the end. On the contrary, he emphatically disclaimed any knowledge of such things and refused to interfere with things that belong exclusively to God the Father:[20] "No one knows, however, when that day or hour will come—neither the angels in heaven, nor the Son; only the Father knows" (Mark 13:32).

Jesus resisted the apocalyptic challenge to provide external signs for identifying the kingdom (Mark 8:11–12; Luke 17:20). And, above all, he would not surrender to the underlying nationalism of much apocalyptic dreaming. Instead, he proclaimed the universal kingdom of God, with nations coming from north and south and peoples from east and west, reversing all expectations and pious speculations (Matt. 8:11–12; 12:41–42; Luke 11:31–32; 13:28–29).

THE APOCALYPTIC DISCOURSE

One of the most controversial sections of the Gospels is the apocalyptic discourse, a collection of sayings about the future, concentrated in the parallel chapters of Matthew 24, Mark 13, and Luke 21. These sections have been called the Little Apocalypse because of the concentration of apocalyptic language, images, and themes. Linguistic studies show that the vocabulary includes words and expressions not consistent with the Gospel in question. Thus, apocalypticists have proposed that the discourse belongs to a separate source of the Jesus tradition.[21] On the other hand, other studies conclude that these sections also contain some undeniably authentic expressions from Jesus as well as concepts consistent with the rest of these Gospels.[22] Predictions about the future are interspersed with events—the destruction of the Temple, the fall of Jerusalem, and the persecution of the Christian community—taking place years after Jesus' death; cataclysms recurring in nature and history; and other events belonging to the end time—the coming of the Son of man and the consummation of the kingdom of God. The most puzzling of all is the mysterious oracle of Mark 13:30 (//Matt. 24:34// Mark 9:1): "Truly, I say to you, this generation will not pass away before all these things take place." What are "all these things"? Who are included in "this generation"?[23] Was Jesus mistaken? Or were the evangelists of the early church mistaken in the handling and understanding of the Jesus tradition? Or are we mistaken in the questions, answers, and interpretations that we bring to this material today?

It seems evident that the apocalyptic discourse is a collection of diverse material all based, however, on references to the future, in apocalyptic language. Despite the complexity of these passages, and that there are no final conclusions for all the questions, at least six different common factors have been identified:

1. Prophecies of the *future destruction* of Jerusalem (Mark 13:14–20; Matt. 24:15–22; Luke 21:20–24).

2. Warnings about imminent trials and *persecutions of Christians*, from both pagans and Jewish authorities, which reflect the situation of the early church at the time of the writing of the Gospels (Mark 13:9–13; Matt. 24:9–13; Luke 21:12–19).

3. Warnings about *false prophets* and *heresies* that will invade the community, pretending to identify the times and signs of the kingdom (Mark 13:5–6; Matt. 24:4–5; Luke 21:8).

4. Sayings reflecting the traditional images of the *"day of the Lord,"* with its frightening conflicts and cosmic turnovers and destruction, which were common in apocalyptic literature (Mark 13:7–8, 24–25; Matt. 24:6–8, 29; Luke 21:9–11, 25–26).

5. Sayings pointing to the *parousia*, to the coming of the Son of man, entangled with other apocalyptic images and language, referring to the end of history—to the final, undatable, consummation of the kingdom (Mark 13:4–8, 24–27; Matt. 24:3–4, 14, 27–28; Luke 21:7, 27–28).

6. *Practical exhortations* to be watchful.[24] The message resounds, again and again, eight times in the chapters: Take heed! Watch! No matter *what* happens, no matter *when* it happens—watch! (Mark 13:5, 9, 23, 33; Matt. 24:4, 42; Luke 21:8, 34–36).

ESCHATOLOGICAL EVANGELIZATION

In our effort to recover Jesus' full proclamation concerning the imminent kingdom, there are a few points that we cannot ignore.

1. *The kingdom will come.* The Son of man will appear. My words, said Jesus, will not pass away. Raise up your heads, your liberation—the kingdom—is drawing near.

2. *This is not the end.* Every single stone of the Temple will be thrown down: never mind. The city will be destroyed: leave it. There will be wars and rumors of wars. There will be earthquakes and famines. Don't be fooled: these things will happen again and again. And they will not last forever.

3. *You will be tested.* You will be arrested, beaten, and judged. Do not worry about what you are going to say: the Holy Spirit will give words. You will be hated because of me and the kingdom. But remain faithful to the very end.

4. *Nobody knows.* There will be false prophets among you (the church is not infallible, it is not the kingdom). They will try to seduce you saying, Here is the Messiah! Lo, the kingdom! Watch out for the kingdom horoscopes and the Armageddon computer games. They will even perform signs. Be on your guard. I told you: nobody knows. Not even the Son.

5. *You have a mission.* Remember, while waiting, there is a mission, to the end of the world, and to the end of time: "You will stand before rulers and kings for my sake to tell them the Good News. But before the end comes, the gospel must be preached to all peoples" (Mark 13:9–10, TEV).

This was Jesus' evangelization of the imminent kingdom—eschatological evangelization.

EVANGELIZING BY HOPE, NOT BY TERROR

Once you disentangle the puzzling collage of Jesus' sayings on the future, what comes through is a powerful message of hope in the midst of tribulations. This is apocalypticism at its best—not to terrorize people, but to raise and preserve hope in the midst of persecution and oppression.[25]

Jesus had an apocalyptic realism about the power of sin in history. He also had an apocalyptic unconquerable hope in the final triumph of the reign of God over all the powers of darkness, sin, and death.

But he was not a consistently apocalyptic producer of cosmic schemes. He did not lose hope in the power of God to work through people for the transformation of history. In this sense, he was more prophetic than apocalyptic.

Jesus had a unique way of using even apocalyptic images and language to convey a prophetic message. Just think of the extraordinary combination of the apocalyptic and the prophetic elements in Jesus' parable of the Judgment of the Nations in Matt. 25:31–46. All the images (Son of man, throne, nations, final judgment) are apocalyptic, but the message is prophetic through and through. Do you want to serve the coming king in his kingdom at the consummation of all things?

There is only one way: right here *in history*, and right here *with your neighbor* in need. "Come, . . . inherit the kingdom prepared for you from the foundation of the world. You did it to one of the least of these, . . . you did it to me" (Matt. 25:34, 40).

Hans Küng, a contemporary interpreter who has strongly emphasized Jesus' futuristic proclamation of the kingdom, concludes from Jesus' teaching that the meaning of the kingdom is "God's cause," "for the sake of man." He sums up Jesus' vision of the kingdom:

> It is not merely God's continuing rule, existing from the dawn of creation, as understood by the religious leaders in Jerusalem, but the future eschatological kingdom of God.

> It is not the religio-political theocracy or democracy which the Zealot revolutionaries wanted to set up by force, but the immediate, unrestricted rule of God himself over the world, to be awaited without recourse to violence.

> It is not the avenging judgment in favor of an elite of the perfect, as understood by the Essenes and the Qumran monks, but the glad tidings of God's infinite goodness and unconditional grace, particularly for the abandoned and destitute.

> It is not a kingdom to be constructed by men through an exact fulfillment of the law and a higher morality in the sense understood by the Pharisees, but the kingdom to be created by God's free act.

Then Küng asks, "More positively, what kind of kingdom will this be?" The author of the already popular and influential Christology, *On Being A Christian*, gives his own summary:

> It will be a kingdom where, in accordance with Jesus' prayer, God's

name is truly hallowed, his will is done on earth, men will have everything in abundance, all sin will be forgiven and all evil overcome.

It will be a kingdom where, in accordance with Jesus' promises, the poor, the hungry, those who weep and those who are downtrodden will finally come into their own; where pain, suffering and death will have an end.

It will be a kingdom that cannot be described, but only made known in metaphors: as the new covenant, the seed springing up, the ripe harvest, the great banquet, the royal feast.

It will therefore be a kingdom—wholly as the prophets foretold—of absolute righteousness, of unsurpassable freedom, of dauntless love, of universal reconciliation, of everlasting peace. In this sense therefore it will be the time of salvation, of fulfillment, of consummation, of God's presence: the absolute future.[26]

If this is so—and it seems a fair résumé of Jesus' proclamation of the impending kingdom—then we cannot limit Jesus to the tormented visions of the apocalypticists or even to the highest hopes of the prophets. Jesus' proclamation of the coming kingdom is the good news of God's absolute future and God's design for humanity. As Georgia Harkness puts it: "The Kingdom is our ultimate challenge and our ultimate hope."[27] The kingdom provides a hope to sustain us in the present and to mobilize us toward the future. It challenges us to be faithful in sharing the good news of the coming kingdom with our generation.

In our effort to recover Jesus' message of the reign of God, we can use Küng's conclusion:

Whether it comes tomorrow or after long ages, the end casts light and shade before it. Can we close our eyes to this fact? The world does not last forever. Human life and human history have an end. But the message of Jesus tells us that, *at this end,* there is not nothing, there is God. As God is the beginning, so too he is the end. God's cause prevails in any case. The future belongs to God.[28]

"The future belongs to God." Good news, indeed!

This was Jesus' eschatological evangelization, and this is the message we owe to the world. Eschatology becomes mission—because we have been sent not as prophets of doom but as evangelists of hope: to announce the coming reign of God! "And this Good News about the Kingdom will be preached through all the world for a witness to all mankind; and then the end will come" (Matt. 24:14, TEV).

The In-Breaking Kingdom

> The kingdom of heaven has suffered violence, and men of violence take it by force.   Matt. 11:12

At this point, there should not be any reasonable doubt that Jesus' evangelization was the proclamation of both the presence and the imminence of the kingdom of God. Why is it, then, that kingdom language has disappeared from evangelization today and often from theology itself?

Part of the difficulty is a misunderstanding of the nature of the kingdom which Jesus came to announce and to inaugurate. This misunderstanding may often be a matter of semantics. What do we understand by "kingdom"? Our generation has a problem with the very concept of kingdom in a time of democracies and democratic ideologies. We no longer have royal kingdoms in the old style, and kings and queens are merely nostalgic conventions in some modern states having long histories, or superfluous symbols to be applied to the "queen" in a beauty contest or the "king" of hamburgers.

On a deeper level, there is the serious questioning of sexist language and patriarchal images, which have for millenniums been used to justify the subordination of women and groups of people. We hope to show that Jesus' concept of the kingdom is so all-embracing and all-encompassing that it puts under question and under judgment any exclusivistic image, myth, language, structure, or doctrine, and declares wanting all of our dualisms, dichotomies, and reductions.

Even more, the idea of "kingdom" is so persistently associated in our minds with the concept of realm, territory, or a static sphere of reality that we cannot grasp the dynamic character of the reign of

God. Practically all biblical scholars and theologians would agree
that the meaning of "kingdom of God" or "kingdom of heaven" is
God's kingship, rule, order, sovereignty, sway, or merely God's
activity or action. That is why many have chosen to translate the
Hebrew *malkuth* and the Greek *basileia* as God's "reign," thereby
avoiding the male chauvinistic and monarchical connotations of
"kingdom."[1]

But even when using the term God's "reign," we tend to hold on
to a static perception of the kingdom as a realm. As we think of the
mineral, vegetable, and animal kingdoms or the intellectual, moral,
and spiritual realms, so we also conceptualize the kingdom of God as
a static order into which we enter or to which we especially belong.
This idea is not necessarily wrong, but it misses the overwhelming
dynamic features of the kingdom as proclaimed by Jesus.[2]

Jesus announced the dynamic, in-breaking kingdom of God. His
evangelization was, then, confrontational.

THE KINGDOM AS CONFRONTATION

The kingdom of God *has come;* it is experience or good news,
centered in Jesus and his ministry. The kingdom of God *will come;* it
is hope, tense expectation, the mobilizing promise projected towards its final consummation. At the same time, the kingdom *is
coming;* in the midst of conflict, it is the center of a tremendous
struggle of cosmic proportions that calls forth a confrontation. All the
forces seem to be released: human, divine, and demonic. The
dramatic climate intensifies as the turning point occurs in Galilee,
and Jesus begins to move toward Jerusalem for the final confrontation.[3]

The arrival of the kingdom produces a crisis. It is like a seed
forcing its way upward through the soil, stones, and thistles of this
world. It is like the new wine which ferments inside the old wine-
skins, increases the inner pressure, and forces its way out to the
bursting point. It is like a new patch in old cloth which tears away
and makes the hole worse than ever. It is like a fire that has been
kindled over the earth; who can stop it? It is like a sword that draws
a dividing line and cuts through the most intimate and sacred
relationships and loyalties, and subordinates any former value or

commitment (see Mark 4:3–9; 2:21–22; Luke 12:49; Matt. 10:34–36).[4]

The kingdom is God's new order. Since its manifestation in Jesus Christ, human orders now belong to the old order. Like contemporary products in a consumer society, they are under the spell of planned obsolescence.

Precisely, because the new order of God is a threat to any established order, the arrival of the kingdom, forcing its way through the old order, produces a more intense reaction. It attracts and repels at the same time.[5]

The kingdom of God "suffers violence"; it calls forth upon itself the reaction of the evil forces, as the magnet attracts the iron particles to shape its own crown. This is the story of Jesus and his gospel. Jesus Christ, the kingdom personified, attracted upon himself all the forces of evil; they crowded upon him furiously, pressed in upon him, and finally nailed him to the cross.

Jesus was increasingly aware of this. He anticipated the struggle, prepared himself for it, and tried also to prepare his disciples for this final confrontation. This is the "messianic secret" surrounding Jesus' journey from Galilee to Jerusalem, the city that was the center and the symbol of all human powers and the best pretender or claimant to the seat of the kingdom of God on earth (Matt. 5:35). Jesus was destined to be a sign of contradiction, a stumbling block, rejected by humanity but chosen by God (Matt. 21:42–44; 1 Peter 2:7).

The kingdom is reversal and, as such, the permanent subverter of human orders. The proclaimer of this kingdom could not expect any other treatment than the one reserved for the subversives in human history.

MAKING OR SUFFERING VIOLENCE

There is a strange saying of Jesus that has come to us in two somewhat different versions—Matthew's and Luke's—which points to the conflictive character of the kingdom in this world.

From the days of John the Baptist until now the kingdom of heaven has suffered violence [biazetai], and men of violence [biastai] take it by force [harpazoysin, "are seizing it," NEB; "are forcing their way into it," Phillips]. (Matt. 11:12)

The law and the prophets were until John; since then the good news of the kingdom of God is preached, and every one enters it violently [*biazetai*, "forces his way in," NEB; "are forcing their way into it," Phillips].[6] (Luke 16:16)

At first sight, in these translations the kingdom of God is "suffering violence" and it is being taken by force. But there is a complicating factor: the verb *biazetai* comes in the variant texts in the passive voice, meaning "to be treated forcibly," and in the middle voice, meaning "exercises its force" or "makes its way powerfully." The exegetes divide themselves between these two alternatives. Is the kingdom making violence or suffering violence?[7]

If the middle voice is taken, the meaning would be: "Since the times of John the Baptist the kingdom of God is forcing its way and demanding a powerful reaction."

The kingdom in this case is both making violence and suffering violence!

Without entering into the exegetical dispute one can take a pragmatic approach, realizing that, in the total witness of the Gospels, both effects of the presence of the kingdom are true to the facts. The kingdom is in-breaking—forcing its way in through persons, institutions, and societies, attracting and repelling, being seized by faith, and being rejected by unfaith. The presence of the kingdom in Jesus Christ is opening its way among the people, forgiving sins, restoring life, creating community, but at the same time exacerbating the forces of the antikingdom that will take him finally to the cross. The presence of the in-breaking kingdom provokes a confrontation and demands an option.

Actually, Jesus invited his followers to "strive to enter by the narrow door" (Luke 13:24) into the kingdom of life: "Enter by the narrow gate; for the gate is wide and the way is easy, that leads to destruction, and those who enter it are many. For the gate is narrow and the way is hard, that leads to life, and those who find it are few" (Matt. 7:13–14; see also Luke 13:24).

You have to choose between options. No one is automatically pushed into the kingdom.

In another moment Jesus dramatized the conflictive and polarizing nature of the kingdom in a world of sin, saying: "It is fire that I have come to bring upon the earth—how I could wish it were already ablaze! There is a baptism that I must undergo and how strained I am until it is over! Do you think I have come to bring peace on the earth? No, I tell you, not peace, but division!" (Luke 12:49–51, Phillips).

The kingdom of God that Jesus came to announce is not only the open kingdom of grace, the joyful kingdom of the final consummation, but it is also an in-breaking kingdom that draws dividing lines and demands an option.

Jesus' evangelization was confrontational.

FACING OPPOSITION

Jesus faced mounting opposition to his ministry. The Gospel of Mark has concentrated the points of conflict at the very beginning of that ministry. Jesus met the antihuman forces which were manifested in those who were "possessed by evil spirits," as suggested in the exorcisms he performed (Mark 1:21–27). Then came the clash with the teachers of the law on the question of Jesus' authority to forgive sins (Mark 2:1–12). At this point there surfaced what became the official verdict of the religious authorities justifying their condemnation of Jesus to death: "He is a blasphemer!"

When Jesus attended a dinner with his disciples at the house of Levi, where many "tax collectors and outcasts" had come together, Jesus' opponents angrily raised the question with his disciples: "Why does he eat with tax collectors and sinners?" (Mark 2:16). They were angry not because of some dogmatic proposition, but because of Jesus' behavior. He heard their question and immediately responded, "I have not come to call respectable people, but outcasts" (Mark 2:17, TEV).

Another point of irritation was the fact that Jesus and his disciples did not comply with fasting regulations (Mark 2:18–22). An even more serious issue was what Jesus' critics saw as a violation of the Sabbath law, how, because they were hungry, his disciples had plucked a few heads of grain when passing a wheat field.

On another Sabbath day Jesus cured a man with a withered arm, and brought the conflict into focus at the synagogue: "Is it lawful on the sabbath to do good or to do harm, to save life or to kill?" (Mark 3:4). Jesus answered himself, proclaiming that the Son of man and the needs of people are above the Sabbath. The atmosphere was so tense that the Evangelist says that Jesus "looked around at them with anger" (3:5). "The Pharisees left the synagogue and met at once with some members of Herod's party, and they made plans to kill Jesus" (3:6, TEV).

This conspiracy to destroy Jesus and his proclamation of the kingdom by words and deeds cover less than two chapters of the story. The shadow of the cross was already upon the evangelist of the kingdom. The in-breaking kingdom was attracting the fury of the forces of the antikingdom.

Werner H. Kelber, who has studied Mark's story of Jesus with particular care and perception, summarizes the situation at this point of the story:

> It is of course Jesus' message and lifestyle which generate the mounting antagonism among the authorities. As his journey continues it becomes ever more obvious that the Kingdom he announces and puts into practice is diametrically opposed to the conventional piety and morality guarded by the authorities. The forgiveness of sins, the primary concern for sinners, the nonobservance of the days of fasting, and the repeal of the sabbath law combine to erect a counterstructure to the traditional ordering of human life. The Kingdom of God entails a new lifestyle, a new sense of priority, a new community. New wine is for fresh wineskins (2:22). The nature of the Kingdom is such that its King is unacceptable to the Jerusalem authorities. A deep logic unites the Kingdom of God and the death of the King. The Jesus who breaks with his opponents by charging them with "hardness of heart" (3:5) knows of his personal ending. Before his opponents have entered into the conspiracy against his life (3:6), he has already anticipated his violent death (2:20). His journey is going to be journey unto death.[8]

Following a brief journey around and across the lake, Jesus was rejected in his own town of Nazareth—by his own people—and John the Baptist was beheaded (Mark 6:1–29). Given this emotional climate, when Jesus sent his disciples on a preaching tour he cautioned them: "Listen! I am sending you out just like sheep to a pack of wolves" (Matt. 10:16, TEV).

Kingdom evangelization is a dangerous business.

CALL TO REPENTANCE

As we see it in the Gospels, then, the coming of the kingdom means a permanent confrontation of worlds. The kingdom is a question mark in the midst of the established ideas and answers developed by peoples and societies. The kingdom is an irreverent exposure of human motivations and of the most sacred rules of human mores. The kingdom is an iconoclastic disturber of religious sacred places and customs and the most radical threat to temple altars, priestly castes, and the most protected "holiest of holies." The kingdom is the appointed challenger of all sacralizing myths and systems and the relentless unmasker of all human disguises, self-righteous ideologies, or self-perpetuating powers.[9]

The kingdom makes violence in the human condition of sin, both in persons and societies. The presence of the kingdom in Jesus' proclamation and action comes as a challenge to repentance (*metanoia*).[10] The presence of the kingdom implies judgment and transformation: "The time has been fulfilled, the kingdom is here, *change your ways and believe the good news!*" Put yourselves in line with the kingdom!

This repentance means more than merely an inner attitude; it means a change of mind, a change of actions and relationships, a total reorientation of life toward the kingdom of God.

As Jon Sobrino has rightly said:

> Jesus' attitude towards sin is of fundamental importance if we wish to understand the relationship between the historical Jesus and the kingdom of God. First of all, his preaching of the good news takes place in the context of a sinful world. Structurally speaking then, the good news must be seen not simply as liberty but as liberation. . . . Overcoming sin becomes the criterion for verifying whether one has accepted the good news or not. . . .

> And the point worth noting is that sin is not seen simply as saying no to God but as saying no to the Kingdom of God.[11]

Repentance is seen by its fruit (Matt. 7:16–19). John the Baptist was right on target regarding this challenging dimension of the kingdom when he demanded cutting the roots of sin and producing fruits of repentance (Luke 3:8–14). Jesus also warned the "sons of the kingdom" that it might be taken away from them and given to others "who will produce the proper fruits" (Matt. 21:43). Repentance goes to the roots in the human heart and manifests itself through actions and relationships. As Jesus told his opponents during the controversy on ritual purifications:

> Listen to me, all of you, and understand. There is nothing that goes

into a person from the outside which can make him ritually unclean. Rather, it is what comes out of a person that makes him or her unclean. . . . For from the inside, from a person's heart, come the evil ideas which lead him to do immoral things, to rob, kill, commit adultery, be greedy, and do all sorts of evil things; deceit, indecency, jealousy, slander, pride, and folly—all these evil things come from inside a person and make him unclean. (Mark 7:14–15, 21–23; Matt. 15:10–11, 19–20, TEV)

Jon Sobrino again has some interesting reflections on Jesus' prophetic understanding of sin as something radically personal:

Following the prophetic tradition, Jesus stresses the personal character of sin as coming from the human heart—though we should not equate personal with an "individualistic" emphasis. Jesus does not view sin in legalistic terms as a transgression of the law. He interiorizes the reality of sin, stressing that it is already inside people in their twisted intent long before it shows up in their exterior conduct.[12]

The theologian from El Salvador reminds us that in both Jesus' message and his historical situation, where the kingdom approaches as grace, "the essence of sin is a refusal of this coming"; it is "relying on works," a "willingness to offer anything to God (ritual services, tithes, ascetic practices) except one's own security"; it is the rejection of God as a future that we cannot control. In this perspective "the real sinner is typified by the Pharisee and the person with power."

Repentance, then, means to trust oneself totally to God.

CALL TO CONVERSION

The in-breaking kingdom calls forth a radical change: to turn to God—and to the neighbor! *Epistrephein*, the Greek word for conversion in the Gospels, literally means "to turn around."[13] Paul Loffler has pointed out that while the Old Testament word for conversion, *shub*, means "turning back to God and to the covenant," the New Testament word *epistrephein* is future-oriented—toward the kingdom already present in Jesus and his proclamation. In both cases, however, it is a turning *from* evil and a turning *to* the Lord, *to* the kingdom, *to* the covenant, which finally means a turning *to* the neighbor.[14]

It is instructive to look at the call to repentance and conversion that Jesus made on his way to Jerusalem. The challenge was always to respond to the presence of the kingdom in himself, in the particular situation of the candidate to discipleship, and always in relation to others.

Consider, for example, the young ruler or the rich man who was looking for "eternal life." Jesus reminded him of the old covenant, the commandments related to God and neighbor. When he answered that he had been a good son of the law, obeying those commandments since his youth, Jesus challenged him to take the radical option: to turn *from* his possessions and *toward* riches in God, to give to the poor and to follow Jesus. The challenge was basically to turn to God and neighbor, particularly "to the poor." This is the meaning of "entering the kingdom" or of "following Jesus." But the young man was not ready and went away sad "because he was very rich." His riches were more important to him than God, neighbor, or eternal life. Idolatry and lack of human solidarity were blocking his way to the kingdom. Jesus was also sad, while saying: "How hard it will be for rich people to enter the Kingdom of God!" (Mark 10:23, TEV; Matt. 19:23; Luke 18:24).

A similar teaching is in Jesus' answer to the student of the law who came with the same question about what "to do to receive eternal life." Eternal life passes through the neighbor down the road, says Jesus. To enter into life or into the kingdom is to become a neighbor (Luke 10:25–37).

The Zacchaeus story is one of conversion to the kingdom. Jesus took the initiative in approaching Zacchaeus, who was up in the tree, and inviting himself for lunch in the publican's home. But Zacchaeus had taken the initiative before in looking for Jesus and at the end of that conversation at home, when he made his very specific commitment: "Listen, sir! I will give half my belongings to the poor, and if I have cheated anyone, I will pay him back four times as much" (Luke 19:8, TEV). Jesus did not bargain with his host about the percentage to be given to the poor. He did not ask Zacchaeus to "sell all you have and give the money to the poor" (Mark 10:21, TEV), as he had asked the young ruler. He accepted Zacchaeus's response to the challenge of the kingdom in terms of straightening out his relations with neighbors and society, in terms of economic relationships, and of expressing his responsibility and solidarity with the poor. And this change of economic relationships and the implicit change in style of life and priorities Jesus called "salvation" and integration into the people of God: "Salvation has come to this house today, for this man, also, is a descendant of Abraham. For the Son of man came to seek and to save the lost" (Luke 19:10, TEV). Thus, conversion is not merely a change of religious feelings and a privatist transaction in our souls, but it is a turning toward the kingdom in Jesus Christ and to our neighbor in service. It is a historical movement with very definite personal and social manifestations. Here again we cannot separate the personal and the social. We agree with Jim Wallis when he says:

> The goal of biblical conversion is not to save souls apart from history but to bring the kingdom of God into the world with explosive force; it begins with individuals but is for the sake of the world.

> Conversion in the New Testament can only be understood from the perspective of the Kingdom of God. . . . The powerful and compelling call to conversion in the Gospels arose directly out of the fact of an inbreaking new order. To be converted to Christ meant to give one's allegiance to the kingdom.[15]

CONFRONTING THE POWERS

Like the prophets, Jesus denounced collective, institutional, and structural sin. For instance, if we look at the collections of anathemas on "scribes" and "Pharisees" in the Gospel of Matthew (cf. chapter 23), we will see that Jesus' criticism was not so much of individuals as of the legal and ideological systems they represented, and their effect on people, especially on the poor and oppressed.

> They tie onto people's backs loads that are heavy . . . You lock the door to the Kingdom of heaven in people's faces . . . You sail the seas and cross whole countries to win one convert . . . You give to God one tenth even of the seasoning herbs . . . but you neglect . . . justice and mercy and honesty . . . You clean the outside . . . while the inside is full of . . . violence and selfishness. (Matt. 23:4–25, TEV, passim)

In personal relationships Jesus could be very understanding and even tender, as he was with the young ruler whom he loved (Mark 10:21) or the good scribe who was "not far from the kingdom" (Mark 12:34). But Jesus could be adamant in his denunciation of a scribal system of religious bigotry and idolatry which was part of a social system of exploitation and oppression.[16]

The same can be said about the legal experts who imposed unjust loads on the people and usurped the keys of knowledge for their own benefit; the rich who refused to share with the poor; the priests who were part of a system of exploitation of the people and who distorted God's purpose for the temple; or the governors who ruled arbitrarily (Matt. 20:25–28; 21:13; 23:1–36; and parallels). And yet Jesus could deal with the persons representing these powers in a very personal way.

Jesus' confrontation with the powers reached the very heart of the Jewish system: the Temple and the priesthood. His dramatic and parabolic action of entering the Temple in Jerusalem, turning upside down the table and stools, releasing the animals, throwing away the coins of the moneychangers, and driving out the merchants is attested by all four Gospels. It has been a puzzling incident for interpreters and followers of Jesus throughout the centuries. Some have stressed the symbolic and religious meaning of this public demonstration. Others have pointed to its social, economic, and political implications in the Jewish context, wherein the priesthood was such an important part of the establishment under the Roman Empire. Finally, still others have interpreted it as one of several rebellions against the rulers, like the one headed by Barabbas and other Zealot groups. [17] In any case, there is no doubt that this was an extraordinarily open and dramatic confrontation, especially considering that it came from Jesus who had stressed assuming suffering rather than inflicting it through violence. It also seems obvious that the religious meaning of the act was intimately related to the denunciation of the exploitative system of the Temple and its effects on the people: "My house shall be called a house of prayer for all the nations. But you have made it a den of robbers" (Mark 11:17; see also Matt. 21:13; Luke 19:46; John 2:16). That Jesus had touched the heart of the system[18] is apparent in the immediate reaction: "They began looking for some way to kill Jesus. They were afraid of him, because the whole crowd was amazed at his teaching" (Mark 11:18, TEV). Sobrino sums up the point: "Sin, therefore, has two dimensions for Jesus. The personal dimension was a refusal to accept the future of the Kingdom of God that was approaching in grace. The social dimension was a refusal to anticipate that future reality in our here-and-now life."[19]

CHALLENGE TO DISCIPLESHIP

It is in the context of the in-breaking kingdom, of the mounting opposition that it provokes, and of the confrontation with the powers that Jesus makes, that we understand better his call to radical discipleship. It is a call on the way to Jerusalem and to the final confrontation.

Jesus calls for total commitment, total renunciation, total subordination of all other values and loyalties—including family, possessions, and life—to the demands of the in-breaking kingdom (Luke 14:25–26, 33; cf. Mark 2:31–35; 1:28–30). Jesus challenged the would-be disciples on the road to break with lesser loyalties and traditions of the past ("to leave behind the dead," "not to look back") and to open up in total availability and forwardness (Luke 9:57–62). Jesus' call becomes what Leonardo Boff describes as the "intimidating invitation of grace."[20]

Beginning with Peter's confession at Caesarea of Philippi, Jesus' challenge to his own disciples is to take the cross and to assume suffering, passion, and death on the way to the kingdom.

In Galilee, Jesus first called his disciples to be with him and to share in the tasks of the kingdom. Now his challenge on the way is to share in his cross. This challenge must have come as a climactic moment for both Jesus and his disciples. On the way he asked them:

> "Tell me, who do people say I am?" "Some say that you are John the Baptist," they answered; "others say that you are Elijah, while others say that you are one of the prophets." "What about you?" he asked them. "Who do you say I am?" Peter answered, "You are the Messiah." Then Jesus ordered them, "Do not tell anyone about me." (Mark 8:27–30, TEV)

Jesus did not reject the title and the confession. In Matthew's version he even patted Peter on the shoulder, saying: "Good for you, Simon son of John!" (Matt. 16:17, TEV). But Jesus himself never used the word "Messiah" to describe his mission. Rather, he used exclusively the expression "Son of man," and not only with the associations of the heavenly Son of man, but with the associations of the Suffering Servant of Isaiah 53 in a way never used before.[21] He began to teach his disciples that: "The Son of Man must suffer much and be rejected by the elders, the chief priests, and the teachers of the Law. He will be put to death, and three days later he will rise to life" (Mark 8:31, TEV).

Peter's reaction revealed that Jesus' disciples had not associated the Messiah with suffering, rejection, and death at all. Jesus reacted as before the Tempter himself: "Get away from me, Satan," he said. "Your thoughts do not come from God but from man!" (Mark 8:33, TEV). Peter's reaction became a direct confrontation with Jesus himself.

Jesus' prediction was precisely his discovery and his revelation: in a world of sin, the reign of God passes through rejection, suffering, and death. Two other times "on the way" Jesus tried to teach his disciples the inevitability of suffering and death, and the need to be his disciple, to take up the cross and follow him in his passion (Mark 8:27; 9:30; 10:32). The disciples could not understand it, and they continued to think of the kingdom in terms of power and privilege rather than service and suffering (Mark 9:33–35; 10:35–45). Three times at three different places, always addressing his disciples, Jesus tried to lead them into the final mystery of the kingdom through his death and resurrection and into the meaning of discipleship in the kingdom.

On the way to discipleship, conversion is not merely a point but a permanent process. And, strangely enough, it is the conversion of believers, not nonbelievers, that is the focal point. Evangelization also occurs inside the community of the kingdom! Peter is a good example of permanent conversion. He needed to be converted to the understanding and acceptance of the cross. There is no kingdom without a cross.

In summary, then, Jesus' kingdom evangelization, in its present dimension as the in-breaking action of God through human lives and societies, takes the shape of prophetic denunciation of personal and public sin; of confrontation of powers and institutions; of unmasking ideologies and traditions; of challenge to unbelief, prejudice, and hostility; and of challenge also to triumphalistic belief. Finally, it takes the form of repentance, conversion, and radical discipleship.

This was Jesus' confrontational evangelization. It calls for a verdict. It demands an option. "Repent . . . and believe . . . the kingdom is coming."

The Eclipse of
the Kingdom

Maranatha—Our Lord, come!   1 Cor. 16:22; Rev. 22:20

Our exploration of the synoptic Gospels has exposed us to the indisputable fact that Jesus' evangelization was no less and no more than a holistic proclamation of the present, imminent, and in-breaking reign of God. But what happened to "the gospel of the kingdom" in the rest of the New Testament and in the subsequent history of the church?

We seem to be faced with what can be called an eclipse of the reign of God lasting from the apostolic age to the present, particularly in our theology for evangelization.

"Jesus foretold the Kingdom and it was the Church which came," said the French modernist scholar Alfred Loisy at the beginning of this century.[1] There is a fact behind Loisy's dictum: the emergence of the church as the visible, historical outcome of Jesus' proclamation, death, and resurrection. But if what Loisy means is that the church was substituted for the kingdom in the apostolic proclamation, then we need to look more carefully at the facts in order to qualify his affirmation.

Was there really an eclipse of the kingdom in the apostolic proclamation? An eclipse of the sun takes place when the moon, in its orbit around the earth, comes between the earth and the sun so that the moon's shadow sweeps over the face of the sun. The dazzling light of the sun is covered by the opaque body of earth's satellite, and daylight appears somewhat dusky; all direct sunlight vanishes suddenly and it grows dark. In a sense, when we move from the synoptic Gospels, the incandescent daylight of Jesus' proclamation of the kingdom appears "somewhat dusky," and we enter into a sort of twilight in terms of the kingdom message. On second look, we may get the impression that the direct light of the sun has been broken into a spectrum of rainbow colors originating from the same light source.

If Alfred Loisy is right, the church was the opaque body of the moon in the way of the sunlight of the kingdom. But, in all fairness, the church was not the center of the apostolic message. The center was Jesus Christ.

Albert Schweitzer, a liberal scholar and Loisy's contemporary, was closer to the truth when he pointed out the other fact, that is, that Jesus proclaimed the kingdom, and the church proclaimed him. Or, as Rudolf Bultmann put it some decades later: "The Proclaimer became the Proclaimed."[2]

What we have, then, is a christological shift, a christological concentration in the apostolic translation of the message of the kingdom.

FROM THE KINGDOM TO CHRIST THE KING

Jesus proclaimed the coming kingdom, and the early church proclaimed Jesus the Christ (the Messiah, the Anointed One, the King). Indeed, "Jesus is Lord" was the earliest Christian creed.[3] The lordship of Christ is the new term for the kingdom (Acts 2:36; 1 Cor. 1:2; Rom. 10:9).

Jesus' eschatological message was: "The kingdom of God is at hand." The message of the early church was "the Lord is at hand" (Phil. 4:5). Jesus told his disciples to pray, saying, "your kingdom come." The believing community, both those gathered around the Lord's table and those repressed and persecuted by the powers of the world, prayed: *Maranatha*, an old expression in Aramaic, the mother tongue of Jesus, translated as "Our Lord, come!" (1 Cor. 16:22; Rev. 22:20; cf. Acts 7:59).[4]

What, then, was the apostolic proclamation—the content of the first generation evangelization? That question has been clarified by the publication of C. H. Dodd's work, *The Apostolic Preaching and Its Developments*. The structure and content of the apostolic message has been termed *kerygma*, the Greek word for "proclamation."[5]

We can find the beginnings of a "factual core" of apostolic preaching in Paul.[6] In his great chapter on the resurrection, at the end of

his first letter to the Corinthians, he quotes the fundamentals of the
tradition "handed on" to him:

> And now, my brothers, I must remind you of the gospel that I preached
> to you; the gospel which you received, on which you have taken your
> stand and which is now bringing you salvation. . . . First and foremost,
> I handed on to you the facts which had been imparted to me: that
> Christ died for our sins, in accordance with the scriptures; . . . and that
> he appeared to Cephas, and afterwards to the Twelve. . . . This is what
> we all proclaim, and this is what you believed." (1 Cor. 15:1–11, NEB,
> passim)

In his letter to the Romans, Paul introduces himself as the evangelist
entrusted with this gospel:

> This gospel God announced beforehand in sacred scriptures through
> his prophets. It is about his Son: on the human level he was born of
> David's stock, but on the level of the spirit—the Holy Spirit—he was
> declared Son of God by a mighty act in that he rose from the dead: it is
> about *Jesus Christ our Lord.* Through him I received the privilege of a
> commission in his name to lead to faith and obedience men in all
> nations. (Rom. 1:1–5, NEB).

This proclamation of Jesus' death, resurrection, and exaltation leads
to the central confession of faith of Jesus as Lord: "If on your lips is
the confession, *'Jesus is Lord,'* and in your heart the faith that God
raised him from the dead, then you will find salvation" (Rom. 10:9,
NEB).

The same *kerygma* appears in the summaries of apostolic proclamation in the Book of Acts, which follow a common outline:

> The prophecies are fulfilled, and the New Age has begun. The Mes-
> siah, born of David's line, has appeared. He is Jesus of Nazareth, God's
> Servant, who went about doing good and healing by God's power, was
> crucified according to God's purpose, was raised from the dead on the
> third day, is now exalted to God's right hand. And will come in glory for
> judgment. Therefore let all repent, believe, and be baptized for the
> forgiveness of sins and the gift of the Holy Spirit. (Acts 2:14–36; 3:12–
> 26; 4:8–12; 10:34–43, author paraphrase)[7]

The reign of God seems to be in the shadow's cone and Jesus
Christ—his life and ministry, his death, resurrection, exaltation,
lordship (or messiahship), his gift of the Holy Spirit, his presence
and coming—is at the center. What has happened? The kingdom
has been personalized!

This is precisely Bishop Leslie Newbigin's interpretation of the shift:

> What is new is that in Jesus the kingdom is present. That is why the first generation of Christian preachers used a different language from the language of Jesus: he spoke about the kingdom, they spoke about Jesus. They were bound to make this shift of language if they were to be faithful to the facts. . . . the kingdom was no longer a distant hope or a faceless concept, it had now a name and a face—the name and the face of the man from Nazareth. In the New Testament we are dealing not just with the proclamation of the kingdom but also with the presence of the kingdom.[8]

According to Newbigin, there is a shift of language but not a shift of subject. The christocentric apostolic proclamation is about the kingdom—the presence of the kingdom with a name and a face: Jesus from Nazareth. *There,* in Jesus Christ himself, is where we have the indispensable and indestructible link between Jesus' evangelization and apostolic evangelization.

JESUS AND THE KINGDOM

After all, to proclaim Jesus as the Messiah is to announce the kingdom. As John Bright has rightly argued:

> If Christ is really the Messiah, this confronts us with an incredible question: What is the nature of the Kingdom? It is an inescapable question. To acclaim somebody as Messiah is to announce that in him the Kingdom of God has come, because that is precisely the mission of the Messiah: to establish the Kingdom. The Messiah cannot be separated from the Kingdom.[9]

There is, however, an eclipse of the kingdom language, and a shift of perspective. We have continuity and discontinuity at the same time. O. E. Evans has addressed this point:

> The difference, however, is merely one of terminology and of standpoint. Our study of the teaching of Jesus has revealed the close connection in which the idea of the kingdom stands to his own person and work. And the fact is that the early Christian preachers were less concerned with repeating *the message of Jesus,* in his terms, than with proclaiming *the significance of Jesus himself* as the crucified and risen Messiah (cf. 1 Cor. 1:23; 2:2; 15:3–4), who was shortly to return in glory (cf. 1 Thess. 1:10; 2 Thess. 1:7). The proclamation of the historical events of the life, death, and resurrection of Jesus corresponded to the

announcement that *the kingdom of God had already come,* and the expectation of the Parousia corresponded to Jesus' emphasis upon the *future consummation of the kingdom.*

Then, Evans makes a suggestion most relevant to our concern: "That the church did not lose touch with the actual terms of Jesus' own message, however, is proved by the fact that it preserved the message in the gospel tradition."[10]

Liberal criticism of the New Testament has, for some time, compared "the gospel of Jesus," as presented in the synoptic Gospels with "the gospel about Jesus," from the rest of the New Testament. Note, however, that what Evans says at the end of his comment is precisely what is happening with the author of Luke-Acts. Luke has presented the mission of Jesus as one of announcing the kingdom (literally, "evangelizing the kingdom," Greek, *euangelizastai,* Luke 4:43) since his programmatic message at Nazareth (4:14–44). The fulfillment of the messianic hope of the *kingdom* has taken place in the *person* of Jesus (Luke 4:21). The book of Acts, though dealing with a different phase and different material, is the continuation of the mission of Jesus—the mission of the kingdom— "beginning from Galilee" and going "to the end of the earth" (Luke 23:5; Acts 1:8; 10:37–39; 28:23, 31). "The affairs of the kingdom of God" were still the subject of the resurrected Lord (Acts 1:3, Phillips).

It is Luke who gives us the consistent evidence of the christological proclamation of the early church; however, it also seems clear that for Luke the apostolic preaching was none other than an announcement of the kingdom of God. To be a witness of Jesus is to be a witness to the kingdom of God (Luke 24:48; Acts 1:8). The fact that "to announce Jesus" and "to announce the kingdom" are synonyms is significant. "When they believed Philip as he preached *good news about the kingdom of God and the name of Jesus Christ,* they were baptized, both men and women" (Acts 8:12).

Luke describes Paul's evangelization as kingdom evangelization. On his first missionary trip, Paul is presented as preaching and exhorting the people of Lystra and Iconium, "saying that through many tribulations we must *enter the kingdom of God*" (Acts 14:22). His months of ministry in Ephesus are summarized as speaking "boldly, arguing and pleading *about the kingdom of God*" (19:8). And the climax of Paul's entire missionary career is when he reaches

Rome. Although a prisoner Paul preaches to his visitors: "And he expounded the matter to them from morning till evening, *testifying to the kingdom of God* and trying to *convince them about Jesus*" (28:23). The end of the story of Luke-Acts, beginning with Jesus in Galilee and ending with Paul in Rome, is a reverberating vignette about the double gospel of Jesus and the kingdom: "And he lived there two whole years . . . and welcomed all who came to him, *preaching the kingdom of God* and *teaching about the Lord Jesus Christ* quite openly and unhindered" (Acts 28:30–31).

We have to agree with Agustin del Agua Perez's conclusion on Jesus' mission of kingdom evangelization: "Kingdom of God and person of Jesus (in the Lukan conception) explain and fulfill each other, in such a way that we cannot speak of kingdom of God without Christ, or Christ without *basileia* (kingdom). . . . Christology is always oriented towards its frame of reference in the *basileia*."[11] This was exactly what Origen meant when he called Christ the *autobasilea:* Christ himself is the kingdom!

THE NEW EVENTS OF THE KINGDOM

The apparent eclipse of the kingdom in the New Testament, however, was much more than a simple change of language or emphasis. As Newbigin suggests, "they were bound to make this shift of language if they were to be faithful to the facts." What were those facts? Jesus' death, the event of the resurrection, the experience of the Holy Spirit, and the emergence of the church. Those were also kingdom events!

J. D. Crossan, reflecting on the transformation of the parables by the early church, interprets this transition poetically when he says:

The parabler becomes parable. Jesus announced the kingdom of God in parables, but the primitive church announced Jesus as the Christ, the Parable of God. . . . There was the *Cross,* and the immediate conclusion was that it represented the divine rejection of Jesus. But if Jesus' parabolic vision was correct, then the Cross itself was not rejection but was itself the great Parable of God. Now, and probably only now, they finally understood what Jesus has been telling them all along. The Cross replaced the parables and became in their place the Supreme Parable. . . . Jesus died as parabler and rose as Parable.[12]

Yes, "there was the *Cross.*" And it was not only a break in human logic. It was a sheer fact: Jesus' shameful death as a criminal; rejected by men—and also by God? It was a stumbling block. An executed Messiah? A cursed Servant of the Lord? The collapse of all hopes around the announced kingdom? The end of an illusion?

Jesus' death was not only the eclipse of the kingdom, it was the clouding of the face of God that had shined in the face, in the voice, and in the life of the carpenter from Nazareth. No wonder that "it was about twelve o'clock when the sun stopped shining and darkness covered the whole country until three o'clock" (Luke 23:44; Matt. 27:45; Mark 15:33).

For the disciples, it was a total eclipse. The daylight appeared somewhat dusky, all direct light vanished, and it grew suddenly dark. "We had hoped that he was the one to redeem Israel" (Luke 24:21). It would take more than a "language event" for the dead parabler to rise as Parable. It would take no less than the event of the resurrection and the good news of Easter morning: He is alive! "The Lord has risen indeed, and has appeared!" (Luke 24:34).

Then, and only then, the cross would become Parable. The suffering and death of the Servant of God would make sense in the economy of the kingdom (Luke 24:45–49). In the light of the resurrection, the rejected man of sorrows shone in all splendor as the "Crucified God."[13] The stumbling block had become the cornerstone (Acts 4:11; Eph. 2:20; 1 Peter 2:5–8). The Crucified One, "offensive to the Jews and nonsense to the Gentiles" had become "the power of God and the wisdom of God," "for those whom God has called" (1 Cor. 1:22–24, TEV). The Parable is the Paradox, the Great Reversal among all the reversals of the kingdom: the Lord of the universe ruling from a cross. The king is a hidden king—the servant king.

And after the resurrection came Pentecost—the experience of the Spirit—and with it, the touch of God's presence, the power of God's healing, the liberating experience of forgiveness, the reality of fraternal community, the joy of celebration, the boldness in witness, the blossoming of hope, and the fruitfulness in mission. The apostolic proclamation was good news incarnate. Holistic evangelization indeed!

The kingdom had come near. The eschatological community felt like it was living "in the last days," between the Pentecost and the

parousia (Acts 2:1–4, 41–47; 3:1–26; 4:1–37; 5:27–32, 40–42; 6:7).
What made the difference was that the message of the kingdom had
been radically transformed because the apostolic community was
living under dramatically different circumstances. The kingdom had
become real—"realized eschatology."

Jürgen Moltmann argues that the resurrection gave the early
church "the reason and the right" not only to carry Jesus' proclamation of the kingdom but even *to transform it*, because the resurrection was a "constitutive part of the Christian message of the
Kingdom."

> They remember Jesus on the ground of the expectations for his future
> which are aroused by the resurrection appearances, and present the
> earthly Jesus of the past in the light of the hopes for his future which
> became possible with Easter. . . . *The raising of Jesus from the dead is
> thus a constitutive part of the Christian message of the Kingdom.* . . .
> The Easter appearances of Jesus are the occasion for remembering and
> taking over Jesus' message of the kingdom, yet they are at the same
> time also the occasion for the *transforming* of this message of the
> kingdom.[14]

PAUL'S TRANSLATION OF THE KINGDOM

This transformation of the kingdom's message is notable in Paul
and John—next to the synoptic Gospels, the two most influential
witnesses in the New Testament.[15] While Paul translates "kingdom
of God" in terms of an all-encompassing concept of salvation, John
expresses it in terms of "life" and "life eternal."[16]

As we have seen, Paul stuck faithfully to the apostolic gospel that
was "handed on" to him, but at the same time he continued to
develop what he called "my gospel," "our gospel" (Rom. 2:16; 16:25;
2 Tim. 2:8; 2 Cor. 4:3) out of his unique experience with the living
Christ, his particular theological formation, his pastoral experience,
and his response to the missionary challenges of his time and place.
He would steadfastly contend that there is only one gospel (Gal.
1:6ff.), but nobody was more creative than Paul in trying to contex-
tualize the one gospel to different persons, cultures, thought-forms,
and historical situations, becoming "a Jew, in order to win Jews," "a
Gentile . . . to win Gentiles" (1 Cor. 9:20; Rom. 1:14–16).

The language of the kingdom appears in Paul here and there, nine
times in seven letters, but it is no longer the dominant motif nor the

theological frame of the gospel message. Sometimes the kingdom is brought about in relation to pastoral problems of Christian conduct—like eating and drinking habits, sexual ethics, social crimes— among his readers. Paul seems to imply that there is a kingdom life style: "Do you not know that the unrighteous will not inherit the kingdom of God?" (1 Cor. 6:9). After a long list of "works of the flesh," including licentiousness, idolatry, jealousy, selfishness, drunkenness, "and the like," he says: "I warn you, as I warned you before, that those who do such things shall not inherit the kingdom of God" (Gal. 5:19–21; Eph. 5:5). One might gather that the "fruit of the Spirit" (love, joy, peace, etc.) belongs to the kingdom style of life. In these passages the kingdom is thought of as an "inheritance," projected toward the future, toward the end, but with implications for the present.

Paul's converts in Thessalonica were so excited with his original apocalyptic preaching on the parousia—so taken by the images of resurrection, glory, and rapture—that they abandoned family or social responsibilities. So, Paul, in his letters to them, reminds them that there is a kingdom style of life: "to lead a life worthy of God, who calls you into his own kingdom and glory" (1 Thess. 2:12), to "be made worthy of the kingdom of God, for which you are suffering" (2 Thess. 1:5).

Sometimes Paul points to the kingdom as a transcending reality which cannot be reduced to manners and conduct: "the kingdom of God does not consist in talk but in power" (1 Cor. 4:20); "the kingdom of God is not food and drink but righteousness and peace and joy in the Holy Spirit" (Rom. 14:17). A transcendent reality and a present experience—both at the same time. In fact, the Christian experience is described as being transferred, here and now, to the kingdom of Christ: "[The Father] has delivered us from the domination of darkness and transferred us to the kingdom of his beloved Son, in whom we have redemption, the forgiveness of sins" (Col. 1:13–14). The forgiveness of sins, so central in Jesus' announcement of the kingdom and in the apostolic proclamation in the book of Acts, is here again as a concrete expression of the kingdom presence.

Here the kingdom is referred to as the kingdom "of the Son." But in 1 Corinthians' great chapter on the resurrection the idea of a

present, provisional kingdom of the Son is presented in the context
of the final consummation:

> Then comes the end, when he delivers the kingdom to God the Father
> after destroying every rule and every authority and power. For he must
> reign until he has put all his enemies under his feet. The last enemy to
> be destroyed is death. . . . When all things are subjected to him, then
> the Son himself will also be subjected to him who put all things under
> him, that God may be everything to every one. (1 Cor. 15:24–26, 28)

The kingdom is present—Christ is reigning—but it is still in the
future, when all evil will be conquered and God will be all in all. We
live in the light of the resurrection and in the hope of the coming
kingdom.

Paul is familiar with the language of the kingdom, but why is it not
his dominant perspective as it was in Jesus' message in the Gospels?
Why this eclipse of the kingdom motif? There are speculations about
Paul's knowledge of Jesus' teachings and of his familiarity with the
materials that became part of the Gospels.[17] There are suggestions
that Paul avoided the kingdom terminology in proclaiming the gospel in the non-Palestinian world for tactical reasons—a lack of familiarity among the Greeks with the Old Testament hope of the kingdom, the risk of being misinterpreted among the Romans for the
political implications of the kingdom language and Jesus' execution
as a pretender king.[18]

THE RISKS OF CONTEXTUALIZATION

There is no doubt that in the apostolic proclamation we face the
need and the risk of contextualizing the gospel to a given time and
place. The question is not only one of language and thought-forms
but of faithfulness to the original message and to the totality of its
meaning.

We have no space to deal with two other important apostolic
translations (apostolic generation) that became part of the New
Testament: the Johannine literature and the book of Revelation.
Without losing sight of the eschatological, future-oriented hope of
the consummation, the emphasis in John is put on the present
dimension of the kingdom as life eternal—already experienced. It
seems that this was the appropriate method for communicating
Jesus' message to Gnostic-influenced (Hellenistic or Jewish) au-

diences. In Revelation, when the Christians are under repression and persecution by Rome, the present experience is described in underground code language, using apocalyptic concepts and images. Hopes are projected to the final consummation of the kingdom, when the Crucified One, the Lamb of God, will assume the universal throne and all the powers of death and the antikingdom will be destroyed. This last book of the New Testament is the one that fully takes up the kingdom theme in an apocalyptic key.

Two things can be learned from this. First, although there is no kingdom language in other parts of the New Testament, we can still look at them from a kingdom perspective. We can analyze Paul's tremendously rich gospel in the light of the three dimensions of the kingdom: past, present, and future. For Paul, as for the other apostolic messengers, the kingdom, the new order of God, *has already come* in Jesus Christ, in his incarnation, his death and resurrection. The kingdom *is here*, as experience, in the Spirit, its gifts and fruits; in the struggles against "the flesh," "the world," "sin," and "the powers." And the kingdom *will come*, with the final coming of the Lord, when "God will be all in all." Paul's concept of salvation is equally multidimensional: past atonement, present justification, future glorification. "In Christ" we live, we die, we are raised and exalted. In the midst of this all-embracing reality we live by faith (toward the past work of God in Christ), by hope (toward the future consummation), and by love (toward present relationships). [19]

Some years ago John Knox pointed to the fact that the expression "in Christ" in Paul's theology is equivalent to "Spirit," "love," "community," "church," and "kingdom of God"! By them, "he refers to the fact that he has, by God's mercy, been made part of that ultimate, eschatological order, that divine community of love, which in the gospel is called the kingdom of God, and which is already, proleptically and partially present among us in the church." [20]

Second, we need to notice that Paul's version of the gospel—which to our knowledge was the first New Testament material written—has been kept with the material that became the synoptic Gospels. The early church perceived what should be obvious to all of us—that Paul's message in his occasional and circumstantial letters and, in general, the apostolic proclamation of Christ, would make no sense without the Gospels and the substance of Jesus'

proclamation of the kingdom. Under the direction of the Holy Spirit
the early church retained the "Jesus tradition," the apostolic preaching, and all the diverse and converging witnesses of the New Testament. All of them together provide the foundation for the gospel we
are called to announce.

This is what makes today's eclipse of the kingdom in the theology
for evangelization, and in the evangelistic message, more painful
and serious. In our own contextualization of the gospel we have not
only built up our evangelistic theology from an exclusively Pauline
perspective or from a purely apocalyptic world view, but we have
also lost sight of the kingdom perspective and content.

THE SUBVERSIVE MEMORY OF JESUS

Here is something to be pondered: the early church was translating and contextualizing the good news, while at the same time
acting as the custodian of the tradition. *Translation* and *tradition*
went hand in hand—a pattern of faithfulness in contextualization
that should be the norm for the church in any time or any place. As
"a treasure in earthen vessels" the church was keeping and making
alive "the subversive memory of Jesus" which would subvert the
world and the church itself!

It is time for us, in the process of translating the good news for our
contemporary world, to go to the sources of our original tradition on
the kingdom of God and to look afresh from its perspective at our
evangelistic responsibility.

The eclipse has occurred as the result of another process: the
reduction of the original, all-encompassing message of the kingdom.
What has happened is that we have reduced the reign of God to
one of its aspects, and we have taken this part for the whole. We
have more than forgotten the message of the kingdom—we have
distorted it.

Sometimes, like some church fathers in the Middle Ages, we have
reduced the kingdom to a transcendent sphere outside the realities
of this world and the struggles of history. At other times we have
reduced the kingdom to the institutional and visible kingdom of the
church. At still other times we have recovered the apocalyptic facet
of the kingdom and preached a catastrophic end of this world with an
imminent second coming. Or we have taken refuge in a reduced

kingdom of our inner experience of salvation or the baptism of the Holy Spirit, without any reference to Christ's lordship over the totality of life or to the social and cosmic dimensions of the kingdom of God. Or we have reduced the eschatological kingdom announced by Jesus Christ to a historical kingdom identified with a particular scheme of revolution or social order. And all the time we have identified our reduction of the kingdom with the whole, at the cost of the other dimensions.[21]

But the totality of the kingdom is there, like the sun within the shadow cone of our particular angle of vision. And sooner or later it will shine. Forgotten dimensions of the kingdom will appear again, as we have seen through the history of Christian movements of reform, renewal, and awakenings.[22]

Not only is the "subversive memory of Jesus" in the Scriptures, confronting and challenging us again and again, but the Holy Spirit is also pricking and leading us to respond in a creative and faithful way to the new challenges and needs of our mission in the world, in the changing contexts of time and space. The Holy Spirit is the other "subverter" promised by Jesus, whose ministry is specifically to awaken us, to help us *to remember*, not to forget the message that has been entrusted to us in Jesus Christ. The work of the Holy Spirit in the community of the kingdom is specifically anamnesis, antiamnesic, as Jesus said: "These things I have spoken to you, while I am still with you. But the Counselor, the Holy Spirit, whom the Father will send in my name, he will teach you all things, and *bring to your remembrance* all that I have said to you" (John 14:25–26).

That time has come: the Scripture with the "subversive memory of Jesus," and the Holy Spirit with its antiamnesic ministry—the two great subverters of history and the church—are calling us to recover the fullness of the biblical gospel of the kingdom to be announced to our generation.

Announcing the Kingdom as Gift

Forgiveness is at the center of redemption, at the gates of the kingdom.

Jesus announced the kingdom as grace—as gift from the Father—through proclamation, through storytelling, through acts of healing and forgiveness, and through parabolic actions such as the open table for public sinners, offering his flesh and blood at the Last Supper, and the final parable of his own death on the cross.

How do we announce the kingdom as gift today?

TELLING THE STORY

The kingdom of God has come! It is not only promise and hope—it has become event and experience. The kingdom of God is not merely an idea or a faceless concept. It has a face and a name: Jesus Christ.

Since the coming of Jesus Christ the kingdom of God has become part of our history, and it has taken the shape of a story. To announce the kingdom as gift today, and in every generation since Jesus came, is to tell the "old, old story of Jesus and his love"—the story of his life and proclamation, of his teaching and healing ministry, of his passion, death, and resurrection. It is to tell the story with the joyful affirmation that: "This Jesus, whom you crucified, is the one that God has made Lord and Messiah! . . . God poured out on him the Holy Spirit and power. He went everywhere, doing good and healing all who were under the power of the Devil, for God was with him" (Acts 2:36; 10:38, TEV).

The story then becomes the good news—the gospel. And we are called to address our generation, as Peter spoke to his own generation in Jerusalem: "You know the message [God] sent to the people of Israel, proclaiming the Good News of peace through Jesus Christ, who is Lord of all" (Acts 10:36, TEV).

In order for this to be possible we have to tell the story. As Gabriel Fackre has said in his book on evangelism, *Do and Tell:* "If we are to get the story *out,* we must get the story *straight."* Which means that we need to know the story, to recover the fullness of the story, and to tell it in terms of our contemporary generation.[1] It was because the story was good news that it was remembered, told and retold, written, passed on, and finally incorporated in what we know as the *Gospels.*[2]

We need also to tell it, to pass it on, to make it real and accessible for every person in this world. The church becomes an instrument as well as part of the story. Christians become living letters and new chapters of the story. The church is the environment of the story, "the storyland" (Fackre's term); the community of the "storybook" is the Bible; and we are the "storytellers."[3]

Fackre has put the story in systematic theological form and in contemporary language. This is valuable to present-day evangeliza-tion because, as he says in his last work, *The Christian Story*:

> It is important for the Christian community to get the Story straight also because the world is aggressively telling its own tale. Assailed by its messages from every side, it is tempting to believe they are true: that we live on the "mean streets" of the violent and promiscuous film or in the vapid bourgeois suburb of the television commercial, or that we await the impending holocaust without hope in God, on the one hand, or on the other, that we can confidently expect that the virtue and wisdom of the race assures upward mobility for all toward a Disneyland of joy and plenty.

> To these half-truths and full fictions must be juxtaposed another sce-nario. It will be strange to the ears and eyes of modernity, a counter-word and counter-vision. The task of Christian Storytelling is to keep alive the set of counter-perceptions so the Church may be what it is and see what it is called to see, rather than be made over in the image of the regnant culture.[4]

In May 1980, Christians from one hundred countries, repre-senting the wide variety of Christian churches within and outside of the World Council of Churches, met in Melbourne to deal with the evangelistic and missionary concerns of the churches under the theme, "Your Kingdom Come." Section III, dealing with "The

Church as Witness to the Kingdom," reaffirmed loudly and clearly the importance of telling the story:

> The proclamation of the word of God is one such witness, distinct and indispensable. The story of God in Christ is the heart of all evangelism, and this story has to be told, for the life of the present church never fully reveals the love and holiness and power of God in Christ. The telling of the story is an inescapable mandate for the whole church; word accompanies deed as the kingdom throws its light ahead of its arrival and men and women seek to live in that light.[5]

This has been the strength of the Protestant tradition with its emphasis on the preaching of the Word, and the printing and distribution of the written Word of God, the Bible. It is today still one of the strong points of contemporary evangelization.

ANNOUNCING GRACE

The kingdom of grace, as available present salvation, is the heart of the good news. This is what we have called "evangelical evangelization"—not limiting this word only to the particular Protestant stream called "evangelical" in the United States,[6] but taking "evangelical" in the more inclusive and positive connotation of the Reformation witness: salvation by grace, justification by faith, conversion to Christ—*sola gratia, sola fide, sola Scriptura.* "Evangelical" means, literally, "rooted in the evangel." It is interesting that the post–Vatican II Roman Catholic church has been incorporating "evangelical" into its own vocabulary when referring to what belongs essentially to the gospel. Evangelical is synonymous with good news.

We have not been free of falling into one of the two extremes: (1) shifting to a "cheap grace" kind of evangelism, that knows only of the gifts but nothing of the demands of the gospel; or (2) shifting to a "costly grace" which does not necessarily emphasize the demands of discipleship in the kingdom, but rather the demands of a particular ecclesiastical tradition, confessional creed, or even a cultural form of Christianity. Thus the good news can be and often is transformed into a new law and an intolerable burden. Moreover, we sometimes tend to preach repentance as a magic key or human work that will automatically produce forgiveness and salvation, more in the style of John the Baptist than of Jesus' proclamation.

We must announce grace as grace, although this may sound redundant. We, as evangelists, have no right to place burdens that God does not put on people, nor to confuse evangelization with proselytizing. Jesus' warning to the Pharisees should apply to any evangelist in the kingdom: "How terrible for you . . . hypocrites! You sail the seas and cross whole countries to win one convert; and when you succeed, you make him twice as deserving of going to hell as you yourselves are" (Matt. 23:15, TEV).

Juan Luis Segundo, a Jesuit theologian from Uruguay, also says something that at first sounds redundant, but which is essential in sharing the gospel of grace: "To evangelize is to announce the good news *as* good news."[7] This is not only true in terms of our verbal proclamation but in terms of our attitudes and relationships with others, both as individual Christians and as churches. Do we reflect the acceptance of grace or the rejection of the law? In our churches do we develop structures of grace or structures of division and separation from outsiders?

PROCLAIMING FORGIVENESS

Jesus came announcing forgiveness as the first gift and sign of the kingdom. His initial greeting to the paralyzed man was "Take heart, my son; your sins are forgiven" (Matt. 9:2). His farewell word to the adulterous woman was "Neither do I condemn you; go, and do not sin again" (John 8:11). "I came not to call the righteous, but sinners" (Matt. 9:13) was his rationale for what he did. To Peter he promised "the keys of the kingdom," and later on he empowered all of his disciples to proclaim forgiveness, to bind and unbind on earth what would be bound and unbound in heaven (Matt. 16:19; John 17:18).

Why was forgiveness so essential? Why was it called "the keys of the kingdom"? After receiving the Holy Spirit at Pentecost and telling the story of God's action in Jesus Christ, the apostles opened the door of the kingdom with the final call and promise: "Repent, and be baptized every one of you in the name of Jesus Christ for the forgiveness of your sins; and you shall receive the gift of the Holy Spirit. For the promise is to you and to your children and to all that are far off, every one whom the Lord our God calls to him" (Acts 2:38-39).

Why was forgiveness the focus of kingdom evangelization? Because sin distorts creation and ruins human life. Sin is the barrier separating us from God, from neighbor, from nature, from oneself, and from life itself. We live in a state of alienation because of sin. Only divine forgiveness can liberate us from this alienation and loosen sin's grip on us. The kingdom of God, as Krister Stendahl said in Melbourne, "expresses the full range of God's redemption, the redeeming, the healing, the mending of creation."[8] Forgiveness is at the center of redemption, at the gates of the kingdom.

This may not appear to be true in our world today. In 1973, Karl Menninger wrote a book called *Whatever Became of Sin?* Apparently there was no place for sin in our contemporary psychology and society. Albert Outler, in his penetrating book on evangelism in the Wesleyan spirit, suggests that modern conscience is no longer dominated by a sense of guilt, as is assumed by our evangelization.[9] Yet sin is real, and the effects of sin are more evident than ever. Maybe in our "permissive" and "post-permissive" society many people do not feel a sense of guilt based on mores which they consider obsolete. Guilt is still there, however, even though it may appear as stress or a sense of emptiness, as frustration or fear, paranoia or cynicism, restlessness or apathy. A few years ago, Henri J. M. Nouwen, in his perceptive book on ministry in contemporary society, *The Wounded Healer,* described what he called the "nuclear man"—the rootless and fatherless young generation—and then suggested that *shame* was replacing *guilt.* He said:

> This fearful generation which rejects its fathers and quite often rejects the legitimacy of every person or institution that claims authority, is facing a new danger: becoming captive to itself. . . . Instead of the father, the peer becomes the standard.

> But the tyranny of the fathers is not the same as the tyranny of one's peers. Not following fathers is quite different from not living up to the expectations of one's peers. The first means disobedience; the second, nonconformity. The first creates guilt feelings; the second, feelings of shame. In this respect there is an obvious shift from a guilt culture to a shame culture.[10]

Call it guilt or shame, the fact is that this feeling does not allow us to be fully human, to be free and creative, to be healthy and strong, to be hopeful and loving. Like the paralyzed man on his mat, we need the liberating word: "My son, my daughter, your sins are forgiven." Or as Paul Tillich put it: "You are accepted . . . simply accept the fact that you are accepted."[11]

This need is not only essential to our personal lives, but to our interpersonal relationships as well. No home life, no community life, no church life is possible without the grace of forgiveness. Furthermore, forgiveness is essential for the life of societies, for the dimension of grace in public life and in international relationships, and for new beginnings.

During my prison experience, when I was submitted to long interrogations the intelligence officer, angry about the church being involved in the defense of human rights, the denunciation of injustices, and work among the poor peasants, put to me a very theological question: "Monsignor," as sometimes he called me, "what is for you the role of the church: conciliatory, subversive, or just ecclesiastic?" I had something to say about each one of these alternatives, but I began with the first handle he offered me. Since he posed a theological question I gave him a theological answer: "Sure, the church has a role of reconciliation. The forgiveness of sins is not only a personal or interpersonal reality, but it has also a social dimension. Any society needs forgiveness and new beginnings. Particularly our own Bolivian society, with a long history of revolutions and bloody confrontations, of repression, exile and torture, needs to break with the vicious, infernal circle of vengeance and revenge. We cannot continue devouring each other like cannibals."

I knew what I was talking about. While in prison a paramilitary fellow prisoner, who had tremendous hate in his soul because of the tortures his military father had suffered, told me of how some top military authorities had been humiliated by a revolutionary movement many years ago when they were young cadets in the military academy. Today they were inflicting on their political enemies the same sort of humiliation and violence to which they had been subjected.

This time the officer agreed with me and said: "That is right, and that has been the humanitarian charisma of the church."

Certainly the church lives by forgiveness and is called to proclaim forgiveness to persons and to societies. One of the troubles of our world today is that many leaders and decision makers act out of hate, resentment, arrogance, pride, and ideological fanaticism rather than by grace and hope. Not only the terrorists and the Idi Amins of this world, who leave behind them a bloody track and an inheritance of hate and chaos; not only the angry Irish revolutionaries, ready to die of hunger or to kill in anger; but many other leaders of better reputation and greater power are ready to bomb neighbor countries, to strike back and shoot down planes from foreign nations without declaring war, or to prepare a first strike in a nuclear holocaust. What can we say of religious leaders swearing vengeance and executing hundreds of their own people for "the good" of their own party as we have heard of in Iran?

Without forgiveness, life is not life and this world may go to its final annihilation. Forgiveness is the door of entrance to the kingdom of God.

DEFENDING LIFE

How do we announce the kingdom of life in a world of suffering and death? Jesus sent his disciples to restore life as he had done; and healing accompanied the apostles' proclamation of the good news (Acts 3:1–10; 5:15–16; 8:5–7; 9:33–34; 14:8–11; 19:11–12).

Throughout history the church has always expressed its concern for human life by caring for the sick and protecting women, handicapped children, and the elderly. The church has used the resources of modern science and medicine in each time and place. It has particularly used its specific resources of prayer and love. Mother Teresa is only one contemporary expression of that long-lasting concern for all human beings up to the moment of their death. In such persons the church has been and always will be *conservative* in the true sense of *conserving* life and the human quality of life, doing this not only out of humanitarian feelings or social service, but as a natural way to announce, to share, to make real the good news of the kingdom of God—the kingdom of life.

The healing ministry, then—whether healing through prayer, medicine, pastoral counseling, group therapy, nutrition and mental health services, rehabilitation from drug addiction, or social reconciliation and the defense of human rights, in whatever form—is not merely a secondary social service of the church but also an inseparable part of the announcement of the good news of the kingdom of life revealed in Jesus Christ.[12]

How do we announce the kingdom of life? If there is one thing we are finally learning in this generation it is that human life is a unit, that there is more to healing than people's organs and bodies. There is also the healing of whole persons (their minds, emotions, attitudes, souls), healing of relationships in the family, healing of the group and the community. So healing has to be holistic, restoring human wholeness. The kingdom of God is the kingdom of shalom: of total interrelatedness, of total harmony and well-being, of peace, of wholeness.

Again, the Melbourne Conference was very strong in affirming the church as a healing community in the perspective of the kingdom:

> Our Lord healed the sick as a sign that the Kingdom of God had come near, and commanded his disciples to do the same (Luke 9:1–6). It is a healing of the whole person—forgiveness for the guilt-laden, health for the diseased, hope for the despairing, restored relations for the alienated—which is the sign of the Kingdom's arrival.

As holistic as healing is, so are the causes of illness:

> Ill-health has many roots: oppressive political and economic systems that abuse human power and produce insecurity, anxiety, fear and despair; war and the displacement of refugees; natural disasters; hunger and malnutrition; marital and family problems; unhealthful attitudes towards the body and sexuality; alienation between sexes, generations, races, classes and cultures; unemployment; competitiveness; the division of humanity into rich and poor. Basic to many of these factors is personal estrangement from God.

So, the church needs also a holistic approach: "The churches in this response must commit themselves in fellowship with those who struggle to rid the world of these root causes."[13]

There are many needs and many ways churches can help in the area of human health, and there are other imperative priorities like "the poor, the aged, the refugees, and the chronically ill." Still Melbourne did not forget the normal and essential healing ministry of the local church as a witness to the kingdom of God:

> The local congregation is to be a healing community. The Holy Spirit uses the loving service and open welcome extended by the congregation for healing. By listening to one another and bearing one another's burdens, the despairing receive hope and the alienated are restored.

Those whose wills have been crushed receive new courage in the caring group. Worship and sacramental life is a powerful force for the healing of the sick—especially the prayers of intercession, the proclamation of forgiveness (absolution), the laying on of hands and anointing with oil (James 5:14) and participation in the Eucharist.[14]

How do we, then, defend life in witnessing to the kingdom as gift? Here again we must be self-critical about our selective commitment to life. Sometimes we fight severely against tobacco smoking as a hazard to our health or a discomfort to our neighbors, but we are indifferent to social conditions disrupting millions of human lives, or the arms race depleting human resources, and war destroying human life and values. Sometimes we are anxious about preserving the environment and natural resources for future generations, but then we deal with abortion as a mechanical device, as just another method of contraception, without considering life values and implications. At times we crusade against abortion and against any legal provision for the poor who may need assistance for abortion, and tremble at the mere thought of the millions of not-to-be-born babies "killed" by abortion. Then we ignore the already-born children, and cut resources that might—through prevention of irreversible effects of malnutrition, of segregation, of the depressing conditions of poverty and marginalization—help those born children of God survive. We are far from consistent, to say the least! We may raise our voices to heaven demanding prayer in the schools and attacking the evolutionist theory of human life, but we remain silent about the waste of natural and human resources used to develop new monsters for overkilling all humanity and destroying the earth.

We spend countless billions making missiles that nobody knows where to store (under the earth, under the sea, or in the sky) and nobody wants to have around—for today and for generations to come! Then resources are denied to children's lunches, old people's survival incomes, and more accessible education for the new generations. And paltry sums are given to Third World nations through the World Bank. What kind of "pro-life" commitment is this?

COMPASSION AND THE SINNED-AGAINST

Here is an area where we need to recover the deepest motivation of kingdom evangelization in Jesus, namely, *compassion*. No evangelization is truly Christian unless it is motivated by the deep compassion of the One who "when he saw the crowds, he had compassion for them, because they were harassed and helpless, like sheep without a shepherd" (Matt. 9:36). There is no evangelization, no real sharing of the good news, without compassion.

When Jesus saw the multitudes he did not see them as mere objects of evangelization or as mere statistics of the unchurched—he saw them as suffering people, as "harassed and helpless." This is the way the tiny Christian churches of Asia were looking at the billions of people on that huge continent, when they met in 1977 for the Sixth Assembly of the Christian Conference of Asia and tried to describe "The Asian Situation":

> The dominant reality of Asian suffering is that people are wasted:
> Wasted by hunger, torture, deprivation of rights.
> Wasted by economic exploitation, racial and ethnic discrimination, sexual suppression.
> Wasted by loneliness, nonrelation, noncommunity.

Kosuke Koyama, the Japanese missionary and theologian, in his moving address on "The Crucified Christ Challenges the Human Powers," presented in section II at Melbourne, extended that vision of "wasted people" to any area of the world.

> Affluence and inhuman levels of poverty are coexisting side by side in this world. One section of humanity is dying from overeating and the other from starvation.

> "People are wasted."

> There are multiple reasons for the wasting of people. All these reasons point to the economic exploitation which is going on in our world on both the local and the international levels. There is no doubt that those who are starved because of poverty are persons wasted. . . .

> There are people who in their own economic zone are neither poor or rich. They have something to eat, somewhere to sleep and something to wear, and they may have more in addition to these. . . . They are not starved but they can be wasted. Physical comforts do not necessarily mean spiritual fulfillment.

> There are those who are rich. Ordinarily we think that the lives of the rich people are not wasted. But this point cannot be made easily. Wealth enslaves man and woman. I am not prepared to say that the enslavement by wealth and enslavement by poverty are identical. They

are not. We all desire to be enslaved by wealth but we do not want to be enslaved by poverty. The former is a sweet enslavement; the latter is a bitter enslavement. But enslavement is enslavement. The image of God suffers from different reasons. The people who are poor must be emancipated from their grinding poverty. The people who are neither poor or rich must be emancipated from their "wasting life." The people who are rich must be emancipated from their enslavement to wealth.

Life must not be wasted.[15]

This is evangelical compassion: to see the image of God in every human being whose life is wasted and to be determined to say, "life must not be wasted"—life is the grace of God. Of this substance the true evangelist of the kingdom is made.

Raymond Fung, who for several years has been working in urban mission with the workers of Hong Kong and is inspired in the ministry of Jesus, has pointed out that we need to change our anthropology—our view of human beings—in our traditional "evangelism." He says: "We have been addressing people only as *sinners.* Surely they are sinners, all of them—all of us. But we have forgotten the *sinned-against,* those who are victims of the sins of others." And that is precisely the opposite of what Jesus did, giving priority in the announcement of the kingdom to the poor, the outcasts, the marginals, the "little ones," the sick, the despised and rejected—the *sinned-against.*

We must consider carefully the fact that the harshest words of judgment from Jesus were not addressed to those "sinned-against" but to the strong, the arrogant, the pious, the self-righteous, the supposed owners of the kingdom. Jesus' warnings were directed more to the insiders than to the outsiders.

To the *sinned-against* Jesus' heart went out in love, forgiveness, and gracious invitation: "Come to me, all of you who are tired from carrying your heavy loads, and I will give you rest" (Matt. 11:28, TEV).

Raymond Fung concludes his own musings, saying:

I am prepared to make a bold suggestion: that compassion for people is possible only when we perceive people as the sinned-against. If we look at people as sinners (as distinct from the sinned-against), we may have concern for them, affection or pity, but not compassion, i.e. suffering together with another, fellow-feeling, sympathy. Many of the evangelistic activities of today have little perception of people as the sinned-against. Many are thus void of compassion. We must recover compassion in our evangelism.[16]

OPENING THE TABLE

The open table with public sinners and outcasts was Jesus' major and most provocative proclamation of the new order of the kingdom. This would finally lead him to the cross. The Last Supper, the last in a long succession of open tables—this time limited to his intimate disciples—was still an open table, probably including the women that accompanied the group of disciples[17] and surely Judas, the would-be traitor. The table of the resurrected Lord was still an open table for his apostate disciples, a rehabilitating table for the runaway disciples, invited to become again the apostles of the kingdom.

What is today equivalent to the open table of Jesus in our announcement of the kingdom as gift? Surely that would mean keeping the Lord's Supper as an open table. During ecumenical events Christians, who have been together in preaching, singing, praying, discussing, sharing concerns and resources, eating and drinking together, and sharing the sufferings of Christ in their witness to the world, often come to the painful moment when they go different ways at the moment of the Eucharist or Communion service. There has been some talk about "eucharistic hospitality," and there are a growing number of churches opening the table to their fellow Christians. But we still have a long way to go until we fully recognize that we are not the owners of the table. It is the Lord's Table, and we have no right to reject anyone he wants to receive and claim as his own. An open table may today still be a powerful sign of the kingdom as well as a sign of contradiction.

It is time for us to recover the evangelistic dimension of the Eucharist. Nothing has been more unrelated to our "evangelism" than the Lord's Supper. Have you ever seen eucharistic services together with public "evangelistic campaigns" or "crusades"? Have you ever heard an evangelistic call to "accept" or "receive the Lord" by coming to share in the communion, instead of "raising the hand," "going down the aisle," or "signing a card"? If not, why not? It says something about our witness to the good news of the kingdom that so many denominations can agree on a preacher, a "lowest common denominator" kerygmatic proclamation of the gospel, and they may come together with their presence, their money, their human resources and personal work, but after that they cannot have a eucharistic service together!

Yet the Eucharist is an act of proclamation by the Lord's own institution: "Do this in remembrance of me" (Luke 22:19); "This is my blood . . . which is poured out for many" (Mark 14:24); "This is my blood . . . for the forgiveness of sins" (Matt. 26:28); Take, eat . . . take, drink . . . "and divide it among yourselves" (Luke 22:17). And Paul, in the first written record of the Lord's Supper that we know of, says: "For as often as you eat this bread and drink the cup, you *proclaim* the Lord's death until he comes" (1 Cor. 11:26). The Lord's Supper is an act of proclamation—evangelization! And this was—even before the Story was written—the very first form used to tell the story!

We have made the Lord's Supper into an esoteric celebration for an in-group instead of a public proclamation and an open invitation. One of these days we may discover that the Eucharist celebration every Sunday, or every fourth Sunday, is not just a spiritual banquet for believers but the most powerful evangelistic event in our congregation! Possibly we will risk interpreting the invitations "take, eat" and "take, drink" as the most meaningful evangelistic call for new believers or returning prodigal children.[18]

Surely the open table is much more than "eucharistic hospitality." It means open homes, open churches, and open communities. I sincerely believe that one of the most exciting frontiers of missionary outreach and evangelistic witness is through what I like to call "evangelization by hospitality."[19]

Who today are the outcasts, the equivalent of those Jesus rejected at his open table? Where are they? This is also a crucial question for the evangelization of our churches beyond just looking for prospective members and church growth, as if this was the very reign of God. The question is where are the people who are marginalized—the people pushed to the margins of life, of society, and of the church? The economically deprived? The socially ostracized? Those put down because of age, educational achievement, race, color, sex, or ethnic origin, the migrants and "illegal aliens"?

AT THE PERIPHERY—THE BLEEDING POINTS

Again, the Melbourne Conference was right in raising this issue of mission at the periphery. Kosuke Koyama reminded the conference that the Jesus of the center is always moving toward the periphery, "revealing the mind of God who is concerned about the people in the periphery" (see, for example, Luke 2:7; Mark 2:17; Heb. 13:12). Jesus began on the periphery. At his birth "there was no place for them in the inn" (Luke 2:7). He moved around the periphery with the "sinners" of Galilee (Mark 2:17). And he died on the periphery, "outside the gate" of the holy city (Heb. 13:12). In a very moving passage Koyama continues:

> His life moves towards the periphery. He expresses his centrality in the periphery by reaching the extreme periphery. Finally on the cross, he stops his movement. There he cannot move. He is nailed down. This is the point of ultimate periphery. "My God, my God, why has thou forsaken me?" He is the crucified Lord. . . . Jesus affirms his centrality by giving it up (Mark 15:2; Phil. 2:6–7). This movement to the periphery is calld the love of God in Christ. . . .
>
> The poor are in the periphery. Jesus moves towards them. People who are not poor can be at the periphery if their lives are wasted. Jesus moves towards them.[20]

There are peripheries in the world and in the global economic system, and there are also peripheries in central countries and areas of the world. Wherever the periphery is, there we are called to be. The conference called the churches to solidarity with the suffering people of the world: "In their witness to the Kingdom of God in words and deeds the churches must dare to be present *at the bleeding points of humanity* and thus near those who suffer evil, even taking the risk of being counted among the wicked."[21]

No less than this is necessary if we want to announce—credibly and authentically—the kingdom as gift.

7

Announcing the Kingdom as Hope

Hopes are the genes of biblical Christianity.   Carl E. Braaten

We said in chapter four that Jesus proclaimed the kingdom that will come through "hoping and inspiring hope." Indeed, Jesus lived by hope and died by hope. He taught hope, and he proclaimed hope. He celebrated hope, and he called his followers to become the people of hope.

As we have seen, the hope of the consummation of the kingdom implies also a warning on judgment and the Great Reversal. It assumes personal and collective accountability and responsibility. It means creative and active waiting. It calls for joyous celebration and unfailing prayer. It demands watchful expectation and trusting intercession.

How do we announce the kingdom as hope today?

OUTSTRETCHED TOWARD THE FUTURE

It is only human to live outstretched toward the future. I was touched by one of Carl Sagan's "Cosmos" television programs. He was describing the marvels of the human brain—something unique in our known world—with its capacity to think, analyze, relate feelings and memories, and able to project itself through intuition, dreams, hope, and planning. He spoke of the spaceships sent in 1977 to explore the universe beyond our solar system and our galaxy. He described a small bottle, containing pictures, sounds, and other clues from our world, thrown into space to be found by a hypothetical being equal or superior to earthly humans in some remote point of the universe. It resembled an expanded and pathetic version of a shipwrecked person on a remote island, casting a bottle

83

with an SOS message into the sea. Sagan finished his program with this comment: "It is only proper of a species that projects itself toward the future and longs for communication."

The truth is that not only as a human species do we live outstretched toward the future—all our individual and collective lives are projected toward the future. If we stop to analyze our own everyday thinking we may be surprised to realize how much of it is related to the future: our plans for today; our daily, weekly, and monthly schedules; our salary or income increase and the impact of coming inflation or recession; next summer's vacation and trips; our children's entrance to or graduation from school; our future and that of our children; aging, retirement, and death.

In stretching our minds toward the future we are caught by both hope and fear. This future-oriented hoping and fearing provides the texture of life.

We may try to keep ourselves inside our own little world of personal goals and plans or family prospects, but it is becoming more and more clear to our generation that there is no future for our individual lives unless there is a future for humanity. The meaning of our individual lives is intimately related to the meaning of history. As Hendrikus Berkhof has aptly put it, "the meaning of our life is fulfilled only when we take part in the meaning of history." Berkhof was addressing the situation of Christians who, because of a defective theology, did not know how to relate their Christian faith to action in history nor their hope in the kingship of Christ to a hope for history.[1]

Today the problem goes beyond theological interpretation. There exists the frightening possibility of the destruction of the earth and total annihilation of the human species. With the insane arms race of nuclear weapons being piled up in such quantities that they can overkill humanity about sixty times, and the gloomy prospect of nuclear plants and wastes affecting the environment and life for generations to come, we face, for the first time in history, the awesome possibility of the end of all future history precipitated by the hand of a human being pressing the wrong button at the wrong time. All the talk about "winning" a nuclear war, "calculated risk," "acceptable losses," is sheer madness as doctors and scientists tell us. There will be no "winners," except the cockroaches, mosquitoes, and flies which have the biological resiliency to inherit the earth.[2] It will be, as doctors said in a national symposium at the University of San Francisco, "The Last Epidemic."[3]

Here is where the annunciation of the kingdom as hope becomes essential and imperative. We are living in eschatological times. Today even the nonbeliever can understand the limits and the risks of history. In a time when supposed preachers of the gospel (the good news of the kingdom) have not the bread of hope to offer, but, rather, the stones of the impending doom of Armageddon (jiving too nicely with the multi-billion-dollar armament buildups, the belligerent rhetoric, the military delirium, and the strategists' demonic game), then proclaiming the good news of the coming kingdom is not only a contribution to mental sanity but also a matter of faithfulness to the gospel.

If there is no future for humanity as such, then the common secular hope of immortality through our works or our offspring becomes absurd. If everything goes to nothingness or to the cosmic garbage circulating eternally in space, all our efforts to improve life for us and for others, to project for the future of our descendants, are a mockery: the pathetic game of those sentenced to death waiting for the execution. In this case the hedonistic motto of the old times is right: "Let us eat and drink, for tomorrow we die" (Isa. 22:13). There is no good news—only doom. The gospel is substituted by the antigospel of nihilism, cynicism, or the sinister sadism of the prophets of doomsday.

THE END: THE FINAL DATE WITH GOD

When I left the seminary the first time, I had no clear idea of the kingdom of God and I had no place in my theology for the second coming or parousia. Two solid pillars of my Christian faith and personal theology were my evangelical experience of conversion and my certainty of the eternal life. And the foundation of my faith and theology was—and still is—God's love revealed in Jesus Christ. That was enough. I had no concerns about the future: "to die is [to be] with Christ, for that is far better" (Phil. 1:21–23). My concept of history and its place in God's design was vague, at least until I began reading Arnold Toynbee after I left the seminary. There was no room for the parousia, and the gross literalist images of the second-coming preachers were an offense to my intelligence and to my faith.

When the world-renowned preacher from Ceylon (today Sri Lanka), D. T. Niles came to Montevideo, Uruguay, I was surprised that such a good theologian and ecumenical leader was mentioning the second coming. I asked him what importance a second coming might have when we had had a first one, and Christ is with us as he promised, and was not the coming of the Holy Spirit in Pentecost already his second coming? Niles pointed to my wedding ring, reminding me of the custom of using a pledge ring before marriage. Then he asked: Do you think that marriage is important for those who have pledged themselves as fiancés? Is it enough to have the pledge ring without marrying at all? What is the meaning of the pledge without the consummation of marriage? And so it is with the second coming, or the final consummation of history in the kingdom of God. God has pledged himself to humanity in Jesus Christ, and we wait for the future consummation of his promise. I knew that Dr. Niles was not pressing to impose, literally, the apocalyptic image of Christ coming on a cloud or like Sabu's magic carpet in the movie *The Thief of Baghdad.* I felt that I had to do my homework in this area of Christian faith and vision. I have done so since then, twenty-five years ago!

Yes, we can escape to a private heaven of selected souls, or the individualistic paradise of the mystic, or the final dissolution in the ocean of the All of the pantheist, but this is not the total message of the Scripture and the vision of the coming and all-embracing kingdom of God—a kingdom that has come and is present and operative in our world, in our history; a kingdom that will come at the end of history; a kingdom that is also real beyond history; a kingdom that will justify and recapitulate our history.

> This plan, which God will complete when the time is right, is to bring all creation together, everything in heaven and on earth, with Christ as head. (Eph. 1:10, TEV)

> The kingdom of the world has become the kingdom of our Lord and of his Christ. (Rev. 11:15)

> When all things have been placed under Christ's rule, then he himself, the Son, will place himself under God, who placed all things under him; and God will reign completely over all. (1 Cor. 15:28, TEV)

No less than this is the gospel of the coming kingdom of God. The world will come to an end, but we look to that end with hope. As Hans Küng has said with his usual lucidity:

> The future belongs to God. It is with this future, God's future, that we have to reckon: we do not have to calculate days and hours. In the light of this future of God we must shape the present both of the individual and of society. Here and now.

> This is not then an empty future, but a future to be revealed and fulfilled. . . . It is not a mere future happening, an event still to come, which futurologists might construct by extrapolation from past or present history. . . . It is an *eschaton,* the ultimate reality of the future which is something really different and qualitatively new. . . . We are concerned, then, not merely with futurology, but with eschatology.[4]

ESCHATOLOGY AND MISSION

The vision and hope of the kingdom is the right perspective and the long-lasting motivation for mission and evangelization. I sincerely believe that part of our problem with the theology of evangelization, and with the elusive issue of motivation, has very much to do with a defective (and more defective because it has been implicit rather than deliberate) eschatology. What do we really expect in evangelization? The conversion of all humanity? The expansion of Christianity to every tribe, people, or culture group, or to every village and neighborhood? The "churchification" of the world? The eradication of every religion and ideology originated outside of the Christian church? The transformation of human societies into a new, perfect social order? The formation of small minority groups of authentic Christians acting as a leaven in the mass of humanity? An endless task of "keeping the wolves at the door," holding back the descent of humanity into sin, deterioration, and death generation after generation? The sudden coming, like a final bomb, of the end of the world? What is our sustaining hope for evangelization? It is common for us to proclaim in our evangelistic crusades that "Christ is the hope of the world." But exactly what do we mean by it? What do we have in mind?

W. A. Visser't Hooft suggested that we might say to each other: "Tell me what your eschatology is and I will tell you what your attitude is in relation to Church, state, and society."[5] We might also

say: "Tell me what your eschatology is and I will tell what your
evangelization is."

Oscar Cullmann and Ferdinand Hahn have called attention to the
intimate connection between eschatology and evangelization in the
church: the events of Jesus' death and resurrection and the expectation of the imminence of the kingdom constituted the initial impetus
to move the Christian outward with the good news.[6]

Carl Braaten—after a critical review of the theology of mission of
Karl Barth, Rudolf Bultmann, and Paul Tillich showing how their
eschatology determines their concept of mission—celebrates the
combined impact of Wolfhart Pannenberg's and Jürgen Moltmann's
theologies with their emphasis on historical eschatology and hope.
Braaten's own book is an attempt to spell out "a theology of mission
in light of the Kingdom of God and the emerging shape of the world
today." His conclusion is that the kingdom of God can be taken as
the most adequate starting point for the mission of the church."[7]

For Moltmann the *promise* is the source of *mission:* "the *promissio* of the Kingdom is the ground for the *missio* of love to the
world"; "the *promissio* of the universal future leads of necessity to
the universal *missio* of the church to all nations. . . ."[8] And Carl
Braaten sees in the hope of the kingdom the mobilizing power for
the whole life and mission of the church in the world:

> The kingdom of God is both the foundation of the church and the goal
> of the world. Therefore, we have and we hope; we give thanks and we
> sigh for more. Living in the tension of such a posture, we cannot be
> religious dropouts with an idle faith and a passive hope. The hope of
> the kingdom is an invitation to work while it is day, to be active in love,
> to sow the seeds of the word and spread the flame of the Spirit.[9]

The promise of the coming kingdom is inseparable from the future
history of the world and the ongoing mission of the church. Braaten
continues:

> The universal promise that is signed and sealed by the life, death and
> resurrection of Jesus sets in motion a historical mission to announce
> and celebrate the universal future that has been opened up for all
> people, nations, cultures, and religions. . . .
>
> As long as Christian faith is oriented by the history of promise and the
> eschatological significance of Christ, there will be a Christian mission

in world history. Without its roots in the universal promise, missionary faith becomes indistinguishable from religious propaganda.

The universal scope of the history of promise posits the whole world as the horizon of its mission. [10]

How, then, can we announce the kingdom of God as hope? By hoping. By living and sharing hope. By working with hope. By dying with hope! To be an evangelist is to be a sign of hope, a servant of hope, a minister of hope.

Our task, then, is to recover the full range of the ministries of hope.

THE MINISTRY OF ANNUNCIATION

To evangelize is to announce the coming kingdom, the kingdom of peace and justice, of love and life, the consummation of God's purpose of love with humanity and his universe—to announce the undefeatable fulfillment of creation.

To announce the kingdom as hope is to announce a future which every present takes meaning from, and in which any past is redeemed. It is to live "by the power of the future." [11]

The prophets pointed to the future consummation through visions and dreams rhymed in majestic poetry. Jesus painted the future of God in vivid apocalyptic images, thought-provoking reversal sayings, and unforgettable parables of the new age.

We have to recover the vision of the kingdom. And we have to reclaim the Bible as our book of visions beginning with the primal vision of Eden and moving toward the final and triumphal vision of the city of God, passing through the bold and inspiring vision of the prophets.

In the beginning God created the heavens and the earth . . . male and female . . . and blessed them. . . . And God saw everything that he had made, and behold, it was very good. (Genesis 1)

Then I saw a new heaven and a new earth . . . and I saw the holy city, new Jerusalem, coming down out of heaven from God . . . and I heard a loud voice from the throne saying, "Behold, the dwelling of God is with men. He will dwell with them, and they shall be his people, and God himself will be with them; he will wipe away every tear from their eyes, and death shall be no more, neither shall there be mourning nor crying nor pain any more." . . . And he who sat upon the throne said, "Behold, I make all things new." (Revelation 21)

[The Lord] shall judge between the nations, and shall decide for many peoples; and they shall beat their swords into plowshares, and their spears into pruning hooks; nation shall not lift up sword against nation, neither shall they learn war any more; . . . but they shall sit every man under his vine and under his fig tree, and none shall make them afraid; for the mouth of the Lord of hosts has spoken. (Isaiah 2; Micah 4)

We are as far away as ever from that vision. Today swords have been transformed into tanks with neutron bombs to kill people and preserve property; spears have become warheads aimed toward the major cities of the world, able to level a million Hiroshimas. And yet we are not supposed to deprive our generations of dreams and visions! Because there is only one thing more important than bread and that is hope. Because "where there is no prophecy the people cast off restraint" (Prov. 29:18).

To evangelize today, to announce the kingdom as hope, is to give the people the bread of hope instead of the stones of fatalism and resignation or the hellish fascination with death and annihilation. To evangelize today is to inspire hopes, to support hopes, to give back to people the capacity for dreaming. To evangelize, to share the gospel of the coming kingdom, is to rise at the Washington Memorial to say, loud and clear, for all the nation and all the world to hear, as Martin Luther King, to say:

I have a dream . . .

I say to you today, my friends . . . even though we face the difficulties of today and tomorrow, I still have a dream. It is a dream deeply rooted in the American dream. I have a dream that one day this nation will rise up, live out to the true meaning of its creed: "We hold these truths to be self-evident, that all people are created equal."

I have a dream that my four little children will one day live in a nation where they will not be judged by the color of their skin but by the content of their character.

I have a dream today . . . I have a dream that one day every valley shall be exalted, every hill and mountain shall be made low. The rough places will be made plain, and the crooked places will be made straight.

And the glory of the Lord shall be revealed, and all flesh shall see it together. This is our hope. This is the faith that I go back to the South with. With this faith we will be able to hew out of the mountain of despair a stone of hope. With this faith we will be able to transform the jangling discords of our nation into a beautiful symphony of fellowship. With this faith we will be able to work together, knowing that we will be free one day. [12]

Like Moses looking from afar at the Promised Land without entering into it, Martin Luther King died before his dream was totally fulfilled. But this land, inspired by his dream, had a turning point in the sixties. I wonder how King would feel about his young follower Andrew Young becoming the mayor of Atlanta so naturally that it is no longer news. The struggle for freedom, dignity, and justice continues, and nothing can be taken for granted. But King was able to dream and to inspire dreams in his people, this nation, indeed the whole world. He was part of the history moving in the direction of the kingdom. What will be our contribution to the common dream today?

We preachers of the gospel tend to be contemptuous of human dreams and utopias. Certainly human utopias may mislead and human ideologies may become idolatrous and demonic, but we should not forget that dreams are the gift of God and every true hope comes from God. "It is not we who hope, but God who hopes in us."[13] We should remember what Jesus said about his ministry as the servant of hope: "He will not snap off the broken reed, nor snuff out the smouldering wick, until he leads justice on to victory. In him the nations shall place their hope" (Matt. 12:20-21, NEB).

Actually, utopias may be the secular way to dream the dreams of God, to negate the negation of the present, to affirm "the un-necessity of the status quo."[14] Utopian thinking is the affirmation of human freedom and the passion for the things yet to be. As such, they may be the expression of God-inspired faith. History tells us how the secular utopias and ideologies were born in Christian soil where the subversive memory of Jesus and his kingdom has been kept alive.[15]

This is the ministry of annunciation that has also been developing in the experience of the church in Latin America in the last few years. Instead of preaching a gospel of escapism ("the opium of the people") the church in many places has been inspiring dreams of

things yet to be, awakening the thirst for justice, raising and supporting the hopes of the poor and oppressed, accompanying the
people in its "walking" (caminhada) toward the city of God, searching for "a more human and a more just society," seeking the kingdom of God and his justice.[16] Men like Dom Helder Camara in
Brazil, or Monsignor Romero in El Salvador, and many others have
arisen to share Martin Luther King's style of evangelization, announcing the kingdom as hope, and saying: "I have a dream. . . ."

THE MINISTRY OF DENUNCIATION

To announce the kingdom as hope means, in the second place, to
fulfill the ministry of denunciation—to denounce anything, any
power, any program, any trend which opposes God's purpose for
humanity. It means also to criticize false hopes and illusions—as the
prophets did with the false prophets and as Jesus did, explicitly and
implicitly, with the hopes represented by the Sadducees, the Pharisees, the Essenes, or the Zealots. In this sense the kingdom as hope
becomes an instrument of judgment, a measuring stick applied to
any human situation. No human order can be the kingdom of God.
No revolution will be the last. Any human or social achievement will
be penultimate—only the reign of God is ultimate and deserves our
total loyalty. The reign of God cannot be reduced to an ideology, a
revolution, or a particular social order. The kingdom will always be
"the revolution inside the revolution." We cannot commit ourselves
to a program, to a national way of life, to a dream, or to a revolution
as if they were the reign of God. But we can commit ourselves to the
improvement and the transformation of society for the sake of the
reign of God, in line with the reign of God. We need both the
prophetic distance from any particular order and the freedom to
engage ourselves with the rest of society to work for the common
good.

To fulfill this prophetic ministry of denunciation, however, means
to be specific, to address the concrete issues of life and society, and
to name things by their names, as the prophets did in the Old
Testament in their messages to kings, princes, priests, and merchants, and in their confrontation of peoples, nations, and
empires.[17]

It is a pity that one of the most outstanding evangelists of our

century, when asked to address the contemporary problems of his
nation and government, has said, "I am not an Old Testament
prophet but a New Testament evangelist."[18] There is no such thing if
we look at the paradigm of New Testament evangelists—Jesus himself. There is no true evangelization without prophecy. And this is
part of our trouble with contemporary evangelization, particularly
with highly organized mass-evangelization programs which include
no prophetic words about the situation in each country and society.
This may be a promotional gimmick, evangelical publicity, or religious propaganda, but it is not prophetic evangelization. Our si-
lence may be the countersign of the good news, the negation of
hope.

This is something the churches in Latin America have been
learning in the last decade, particularly the Roman Catholic church
which has been the power behind the powers for centuries. The
church has discovered the poor and rediscovered the gospel. The
church is now listening to "the cry of my people" and is becoming
"the voice of the voiceless." The church has become the most faithful
and serious source of denunciation of oppression and defense of the
oppressed, especially in the countries ruled by the national security
ideology under the most repressive regimes. Sometimes the church
has kept a low profile. Sometimes it has operated openly and pub-
licly, uncovering hidden truths and unmasking government lies;
denouncing terrorism's open violence; and most often denouncing
the omnipresent violence of the system—the "institutional violence" of our societies (which produces hunger, unemployment,
malnutrition, and marginalization)—and calling it what it is: "institutionalized sin."

This prophetic ministry is always costly. According to a French
publication, in the years preceding the 1979 Conference of Bishops
in Puebla, Mexico, fifteen hundred priests, nuns, pastors, and lay
people had been arrested, searched, interrogated, imprisoned, exiled, tortured, killed, or had "disappeared"—precisely because of
this prophetic witness.[19]

Included among the prophetic witnesses raising their voices of
denunciation are several outstanding bishops—Dom Helder Camara and Pedro Casaldaliga in Brazil, Monsignor Leonidas Proaño
in Ecuador, Monsignor Jorge Manrique in Bolivia—who have been

objects of defamation, threats, media boycotts, and other tactics of moral, political, or military pressure. The most dramatic example and the best known in the United States these days is the late archbishop Oscar Arnulfo Romero from El Salvador.

PROPHET AND MARTYR IN EL SALVADOR

Monsignor Romero was a kind, spiritually oriented pastor of the flock, who was selected to become the archbishop because of his rather conservative views and attitudes. But the tragic situation of El Salvador and its people had a consciousness-raising effect on Archbishop Romero and, as he said, "as a pastor, I cannot cease to accompany my people . . . and to accept with them the risks of the moment." He had to speak up for his people![20]

After one month the new archbishop was struck by the assassination of a fellow priest, Father Rutilio Grande, and ordered by the White Warriors Union, a right-wing terrorist squad, to execute all Jesuit priests as communists and to flee the country. Monsignor Romero not only stayed with his priests but took a firm stance in the defense of the rights of the people. He began supporting the civil-military junta in its declared intention to institute land reforms and to make other changes. It soon became clear that the junta was not only unable or unwilling to implement the changes, but that "the brutality was systematic and premeditated, aimed at suppressing popular leadership and terrorizing the entire society with fear of murder, mutilation, rape, and torture."

Archbishop Romero's last homily is a good example of his pastoral-prophetic ministry. In one sense it is very conventional, but in the explosive situation of El Salvador it was like a match lit in a tinder box. He commented on the three biblical passages of the day (it was Lent, March 23, 1980) stressing the personal nature of sin and the personal responsibility of the social situation, and he criticized those who condemn social sin, "institutionalized violence," and structural injustice without realizing the sin in their own hearts. He also stressed the total and transcendent quality of Christian liberation and the unique mission of the church. He quoted the Puebla document, signed by him and other Latin American bishops, denouncing the "false earthly visions" of those motivated by the selfish exploitation of others, Marxist ideologies that reduce man to "a cog in the

machinery," the national security ideology that considers people to
be servants of the state. Then he agreed with the New Testament
texts that law is for man and not man for the law. He called the
people to adhere to an unchanging Christ and be ready to deal with
the changes of society.

But the volatile dynamite would appear in the less-likely sector of
the mass: the announcements! During this period church events
were announced, as well as the names and circumstances of people
who had been searched and beaten in their homes, kicked, raped,
and barbarously killed. Thousands of people came to mass every
Sunday, and many more listened to the radio (which had been
destroyed some weeks before, but reinstalled precisely that Sunday
with ecumenical help). After the report of the last military repression of peasants on March 17, 1980, Monsignor Romero made his
plea to stop the violence:

> The basic question is how to come out of this critical stage in the least
> violent way. And on this point the main responsibility is that of the
> civilian, and notably, the military rulers. . . .
>
> I would like to appeal in a special way to the men of the army, and in
> particular to the troops of the National Guard, the Police, and the
> garrisons. Brothers, you belong to our own people. You kill your own
> brother peasants; and in the face of an order to kill that is given by man,
> the law of God should prevail that says: Do not kill!
>
> The Church, defender of the rights of God, of the law of God, of the
> dignity of the human person, cannot remain silent before so much
> abomination.
>
> We want the government seriously to consider that reforms mean
> nothing when they come bathed in so much blood. Therefore, in the
> name of God, and in the name of this long-suffering people, whose
> laments rise to heaven every day more tumultuously, I beseech you, I
> beg you, I command you in the name of God: Stop the repression![21]

This was prophetic denunciation, responsible, direct, and docu-
mented, out of a bleeding pastoral heart who knew by name the
raped girls, the murdered young people, the slaughtered peasants.
But this kind of denunciation cannot be tolerated by those who are
responsible for what is happening.

The next day, while Monsignor Romero raised the cup with the
blood of Christ at the altar of the chapel in the hospital where he

ministered to cancer-ridden poor, he was killed and his paid assassin disappeared, safe to this day. Prophecy, as happens so often, had become *martyria*.

MARTYRIA

One year later, four American missionary women paid the price of rape, torture, and assassination for their services to the poor people of El Salvador. Other American missionaries have also paid part of this costly prophetic ministry of denunciation, all over Latin America, in the name of the gospel.[22]

Less known, and probably much less understood even when known by their fellow Christians, are a group of creative and daring Christians in the United States who have been trying to name the unnamed and to mention the unmentionable, denouncing at their own risk the whole industrial-military establishment which profits from the continuous buildup of nuclear weapons and the politics of brinkmanship. Before dawn these Christians have entered high-security areas where nuclear weapons are assembled or located, climbing over wired fences to pray at nuclear weapon bunkers, hammer symbolically on nuclear warheads ("to beat swords into plowshares"), and spill their own blood on blueprints or on missile sections. All of them have been arrested, some have already served two years, and some have been sentenced to three to ten years in prison. The article by Ched Myers in *Christian Century* (September 16, 1981) is entitled "Storming the Gates of Hell." The subtitle, "Reflections on Christian Evangelism in Nuclear Security Areas," reminds us of the close relationship between denunciation and the announcement of the kingdom as hope.[23] Are we able to see that relationship?

Of course, this type of confrontation can be as ineffective and short-lived as Jesus' expulsion of the merchants from the Temple. What we need to remember however, is that this denunciation is not merely political agitation but a genuine expression of the proclamation of hope in the reign of God. Though the action is one of confrontation, unmasking, and denunciation, it is still done with the hope of change, in the name of the hope that is being stolen from the people, and which is promised, guaranteed by God himself.

Gestures like the above could be dismissed as an invitation to trouble, a martyr complex. But we never know how God may use the blood of martyrs as a seed for his kingdom. Father Luis Espinal, another Jesuit, gradually moved from his harmless specialization in films and communications to a growing identification with the struggles of the Bolivian people. As director of the weekly paper that had a headline on denunciation of terrorism—orchestrated by intelligence services and authorities in association with the cocaine syndicate—he became the natural target for repressive forces who abducted, tortured, and machine-gunned him from behind. The day after his assassination, Father Luis Espinal's was the name raised as a flag all over the nation by thousands of students, workers, and common people in every city. His death had, in one stroke, erased for a whole generation the accusation that "religion is the opium of the people"!

Martyria is also a ministry of hope. The martyr is the person of hope—even beyond death. Martyr means witness—a witness who puts his/her life on the line. We do not know when the kingdom will come, but we can put our lives at the service of the kingdom, as witnesses of hope. When the disciples asked Jesus about when the kingdom would come, he responded: "It is not for you to know times or seasons . . . but you shall receive power when the Holy Spirit has come upon you; and you shall be my witnesses" (Acts 1:7–8). And this is the heart of Jesus' message in the Little Apocalypse: there will be tribulations but they will provide the opportunity for witness. The promise of the Holy Spirit for witness is inseparable from the situation when the life of the martyr is at stake: "You will be summoned to appear before governors and kings on my account to testify in their presence. . . . So when you are arrested and taken away, do not worry beforehand about what you will say, but when the time comes say whatever is given you to say; for it is not you who will be speaking, but the Holy Spirit" (Mark 13:9, 11, NEB).

The same promise is voiced by the apostle Peter for Christians under trial or social pressure: "Always be prepared to make a defense to any one who calls you to account for the hope that is in you" (1 Peter 3:15).

This was the way Christians evangelized the Roman world in the first three centuries when there were no temples and no campaigns of mass evangelism. But Christians were ready to give account of their hope, even in the midst of torture and death. And a dying world was conquered by this unconquerable hope. Tertullian said that the blood of martyrs is the seed of the church. Have we forgotten this? Do we believe that we will conquer the world just by publicity and promotional devices or by perfecting our strategies and methodologies? Do we really expect that the world will be won for Christ just by cheap evangelism?

THE MINISTRY OF CONSOLATION

Finally, to announce the kingdom as hope means to *fulfill our ministry of consolation*. This is another discovery of the Christian churches in Latin America in the last decade: the ministry to the brokenhearted. Tens of thousands have suffered imprisonment, torture, exile, and violent death in Chile, Argentina, Uruguay, Brazil, Nicaragua, El Salvador, and other countries. The churches have been called to minister to those suffering oppression and repression directly, as well as to their families, to refugees, and to those harassed by the powers that be. The defense of human rights has been much more than a foreign policy device or political slogan; it has become a matter of witness and confession. As the German church had to draw the line of confession in relation to pagan National Socialism, so the Christian churches in Latin America have taken the defense of human rights to be the equivalent of evangelical confession, as the dividing line between the kingdom and the antikingdom. The ministry to the brokenhearted in the most painful and repressive situations is part and parcel of the announcement of the kingdom as hope.

To evangelize in our context means also to keep hope against hope. We should not forget that the hopeful message of the coming kingdom has been proclaimed not in times of peace and freedom but in times of unrest, oppression, and persecution. The apocalyptic literature was born out of oppression and marginalization for the people of God. It was not written to threaten or to frighten people but to raise their hope. John himself, the writer of Revelation, wrote his visions while imprisoned and exiled on the rocky island of Patmos: "I John, your brother, who share with you in Jesus the tribulation and the kingdom and the patient endurance, was on the island called Patmos on account of the word of God and the testimony of Jesus" (Rev. 1:9). John was evangelizing the brokenhearted in the seven churches of Asia who suffered under the persecution of the Roman emperor and his repressive power. But John was doing it from within, as a "brother in tribulation, in the kingdom, in endurance." The kingdom evangelization, the announcement of the kingdom as hope, the ministry of consolation, cannot be made from outside. What does this say to the pretensions of our crusading evangelizations around the world?

The good news of the kingdom as hope calls us to a ministry of annunciation, denunciation, *martyria*, and consolation. No less than this will be evangelization in the perspective of the coming kingdom. But this ministry needs to be holistic in itself: there is no real annunciation without denunciation, no real denunciation without annunciation and consolation, no real *martyria* which is not at the same time annunciation, denunciation, and consolation. A truly holistic evangelization takes the whole gospel—and our whole life.

To announce the kingdom as hope is to proclaim the good news of "the acceptable year of the Lord," the jubilee, the coming kingdom of God, in the midst of the bad news of the world, and to "the poor . . . the captives . . . the blind . . . the brokenhearted . . . and the oppressed," as our Lord proclaimed in his inaugural message. To join with the people in the hope and the acclamation of our coming Lord, shouting in the streets of the city:

> Blessed is the King who comes in the name of the Lord! Peace in heaven and glory in the highest! (Luke 19:38)

> Maranatha—Come, Lord Jesus! (Rev. 22:20)

Announcing the Kingdom as Challenge

Discipleship is the only form in which faith can exist.

Eduard Schweizer

Jesus announced the in-breaking kingdom as a call to radical discipleship. How do we announce the kingdom today as a call to discipleship? How would it resemble what we might call discipleship evangelization?

Actually, we are today watching a recovery of discipleship in the life of the church and in evangelistic strategy. Some years ago, Robert E. Coleman wrote a book entitled *The Master Plan of Evangelism,* which has become a classic manual for evangelism courses and workshops. Coleman stresses the fact that the master plan of Jesus was the training of his disciples. He invested in them most of his three years of public ministry.[1]

Among its many contributions to evangelistic strategy in its twenty-five years of very active life, the Church Growth School, based in Pasadena, California, has also insisted that the so-called Great Commission is essentially a mandate to "make disciples." It is true that the school's understanding of discipleship evangelization may be limited to an introduction to the Christian faith, which enables the candidate to make a quick decision, but the movement has stimulated the personal work of "discipling" instead of an excessive dependence on mass evangelization.[2]

RADICAL DISCIPLESHIP

Among the evangelicals in the United States, probably the most creative and challenging (more creative, by far, than the much-publicized Moral Majority, but with much less political clout) has

101

been the "radical discipleship movement," well represented by the publications *Sojourners* and *The Other Side*. This renewal movement, inside the conservative evangelical new generations, has been very influential in other parts of the world, for example, in Great Britain, Latin America, and other places with a vigorous intervarsity work. Samuel Escobar, René Padilla, and Orlando Costas from Latin America, names identified with this stream, have been very influential in the life of churches and seminaries, and especially, in the Lausanne Congress on World Evangelization.[3] Evangelicals have traditionally been committed to evangelization and its doctrinal emphasis. The radical discipleship stream, however, is less naive about traditional stereotypes of evangelical piety and life style. They have also been strongly critical of "cultural Christianity"—the illegitimate marriage between evangelical faith and the American way of life or American politics. Through publications and community experiments they have tried to respond to the call to discipleship in the kingdom and to engage in costly discipleship evangelization—within and outside of the church.

The same is true of the extraordinary renewal (which they call true evangelization) of the Roman Catholic church in Latin America during the last fifteen or so years, particularly through the phenomenal emergence of the Base Christian Communities. These are grass-roots communities which show a holistic type of discipleship, including common celebration, Bible study, interpersonal growth, and social engagement. It is estimated that there are 150 thousand of these all over Latin America, 80 thousand of them in Brazil alone.[4]

Waldron Scott (the former general secretary of the World Fellowship of Evangelicals) in his recent book, *Bringing Forth Justice: A Contemporary Perspective on Mission*, considers that "the true objective of evangelism is discipleship," which should not be confused with church growth, and that "evangelism should be subordinated to discipleship."[5]

IN THE BEGINNING WAS DISCIPLESHIP

It is a fact of the biblical record that "disciples" is the oldest name for Christians: "In Antioch the disciples were for the first time called Christians" (Acts 11:26). In the book of Acts the name "Christians" occurs only twice, while "disciples" is used thirty times. It is interesting to note that the name "Christian" was very much a matter of discussion more than a century ago in the origins of the "Christian Churches" and "Disciples of Christ" denomination in the United States. Ronald E. Osborn gives the rationale behind those discussions about the name of the emerging denomination under the leadership of Alexander Campbell and Barton Stone:

> Alexander Campbell thought that to call ourselves "Christians" would be a little pretentious. It would suggest that we had already "arrived," whereas if we called ourselves "disciples," it would emphasize that we are still learning, we are following. It wouldn't seem quite so presumptuous as the other title.[6]

Indeed. And this is the point I would like to make. Even if we call ourselves "Christians," or "evangelicals," we are Christians-in-the-making, we are "still learning, still following." We are disciples in the kingdom, followers of Jesus on the way. Incidentally, this was the other name for Christians in the book of Acts: followers of "the Way" (Acts 9:2; 19:9, 23; 22:4; 24:14, 22).

To be disciples of the kingdom and to make disciples in the kingdom is what evangelization is all about. At least this was Jesus' way of evangelization in the kingdom perspective.

Jesus invented discipleship.[7] There were teachers and disciples in the Greek schools of philosophy, and the rabbis in Israel had their own "disciples of God" to be taught the Torah—but a rabbi would never call a disciple to himself. The would-be disciple would seek out the rabbi. But Jesus called his disciples and challenged them to forget everything else and follow him. Further, a disciple of the rabbi might dream of someday becoming even better, if possible, than his master; but a disciple of Jesus could never expect that someday he would be the "Son of man"!

Jesus' discipleship is one of a kind. Juan Stam, from the Seminario Evangelico Latinoamericano of Costa Rica, has made a list of seven distinctive features, one of which is its lifelong character, "Jesus' discipleship was permanent. The invitation was for life. Consequently, nobody could expect to be graduated!"[8]

DISCIPLESHIP IN THE KINGDOM

Jesus' discipleship was discipleship in the kingdom. As Jim Wallis says, "Christian discipleship revolved around the hub of the kingdom."[9] Jesus started his proclamation of the reign of God by calling his first disciples. He called them "to be with him" and sent them "to announce the Kingdom of God" (Matt. 10:7; Luke 9:60; 10:9, 11).

Jesus' discipleship was his model for kingdom evangelization. His disciples would have a taste of the kingdom that had come in Jesus' ministry. They were going to be a sign and an anticipation of the new order of God. They were going to be the witnesses of the kingdom until the end of the world—and of time.

Waldron Scott suggests that while Jesus' preaching, teaching, and healing were only his tactics for evangelization, discipling was his long-range strategy![10]

Jesus left behind two things: the message of the kingdom and a community of disciples. As George E. Ladd has said, Jesus did not leave any other structure: "No separate synagogue, no special place of meeting, no fixed teachings, no new legislation (halachah), no organization. The one thing which bound them together was their personal relationship to Jesus and his message about the Kingdom of God."[11]

Discipleship is in itself an anticipation of the kingdom. Jesus' community of disciples was indeed an eschatological sign. As Ladd also says, "Those who accepted Jesus' message are also an eschatological fellowship in the sense that they have already experienced the kingdom: forgiveness, fellowship, commitment to God's reign."[12]

Eduard Schweizer after almost four hundred pages of careful exegesis of the Gospel of Mark—in which the theme of discipleship runs as a golden thread—concludes that "discipleship is the only form in which faith can exist."[13] Which means to say that Christian faith means nothing less than following Christ on the way of the kingdom.

This may seem an overstatement. But for those acquainted with Dietrich Bonhoeffer's The Cost of Discipleship, the above affirmation will sound familiar. Actually, what Bonhoeffer is saying is: "Christianity without the living Christ is inevitably Christianity without discipleship; and Christianity without discipleship is always Christianity without Christ."[14]

Werner H. Kelber, in his provocative study, The Kingdom in Mark, insists also on the intimate relationship between the kingdom and discipleship: "The enlistment of Simon, Andrew, James, and John into the service of discipleship (1:16–20) from the outset accords a communal dimension to the Kingdom. . . . It consists of people and it bids for people (1:17c)."[15]

"It consists of people and it bids for people." Is not this also the description of the church? The church is not the kingdom, but it is a sign of the kingdom. As such, it "consists of people and bids for people." And what is evangelization but bidding for people? Kingdom evangelization is people's business—it has to do with the totality of life for the people. The church, as has been said, "is the people of God at the service of the peoples of God."

DISCIPLESHIP FOR THE KINGDOM

The church "bids for people" in its evangelization. How could it be otherwise, since the church is entrusted with such good news for the world? Indifference to people, lack of concern for those who do not know the good news of the reign of God, is not a faithful discipleship. The church, however, does not bid only "for souls," but for people, real people who are called to enter into the reign of God—a multidimensional reign that has to do with the totality of life for people.

And the church does not bid for people for its own sake, for church growth. Church growth is never the aim of the church, but the fruit of its witness to the kingdom, the outcome of the ministry to the world, the Lord's free blessing. The book of Acts, *after* describing the quality of life and ministry of the early church, spells out God's gift of growth: "And *the Lord added* to their number day by day" (Acts 2:47).

Discipleship evangelization, then, means recruitment—an invitation to participate in the blessings of the kingdom, to celebrate the hopes of the kingdom, and to engage in the tasks of the kingdom. It means recruitment to discipleship *in* the kingdom and *for* the kingdom.

We need to correct the almost-invincible tendency of our evangelization to present the gospel in terms of "blessings"—benefits to be received, answers to all our questions, remedy to all our evils, new life to be enjoyed, a future state to be secured—without at the same time presenting the challenges, demands, and tasks of the kingdom. We need to remember Bonhoeffer's warning about reducing "costly discipleship" to "cheap grace."

The emergence of the Base Christian Communities (*comunidades de base*) in the most deprived areas of Latin America during the years of major oppression and repression throws a new light and poses a new challenge to the meaning of discipleship *in* and *for* the kingdom. Some of these grass-roots Christian communities exist—like some charismatic cells—among urban middle classes, students, or professionals, but the great majority are among city workers, slum dwellers, peasants, people from small towns, river ports, or on rubber plantations in the jungle. Here is the description of one Base Christian Community in Tacaimbo, a town of three thousand inhabitants one hundred miles from Recife, the main city of northeastern Brazil:

> The vast majority of the people lead lives of doing without, oppressed and afflicted by the vicious circle of poverty which, with cumulative causes, spreads like a cancer. It is members of the [Basic Christian Communities] who describe themselves as follows: "The poor majority have no fixed work; they work for hire in the fields, earning twelve cruzeiros [one dollar at a time] a day. That fieldwork does not provide enough to live, but only to vegetate. That is why many experience hunger. The people thank God when they have beans, corn and manioc root meal. Such "food" does not provide enough to live. They live by moral force; they live because they withstand it somehow. There is meat for one day, but for eight days there is none. Health is very poor. Sometimes a father has five or six children, and four die. They die of need, disregarded, because they cannot be treated. Hence, most of the diseases occur among the children. . . . Most of the people here in Tacaimbo reside in flimsy dwellings, in mud huts. There is almost no sanitation in those dwellings, they have no cesspools. All the children have swollen bodies, and are vomiting with dysentery, which is endless. The school facilities are very unstable. What is learned from them is rubbish. I have a daughter who has been in the school for three years, and she is just now learning to write her name."[16]

Now, these people are Christians. And they are in the discipleship of the kingdom and for the kingdom. They may be deprived of the most basic elements for human life, but they know of God's love for them, of Christ's passion and resurrection, of the hope of the kingdom, and they are beginning to move, "to walk toward the kingdom." They describe their experience of recent years in coming together, mobilizing for the life of their communities, constituting the church that is "born from the people," as a *caminhada* (a "journey"). They hope and struggle not only for themselves but for others. Some of the most impressive—and historical—inputs to the Puebla Conference of Latin American Catholic Bishops were the messages, proposals, and requests from thousands of those small Christian communities.

What is a *comunidad de base?* Actually, it is a discipleship community of twenty-five to thirty-five people, or up to one hundred in a neighborhood or a town. What do they do? There is great variation among them, but one can find common elements with other Christian cells throughout history: Bible study, hymn singing, catechetical instruction, fellowship, sharing of experiences and concerns.

What is remarkable, however, and not so common in other grass-roots Christian groups, is the prominence of the issues of the community and of society in general. Bible reading is related to the surroundings and to the real life and problems of the people. The community sets the agenda: water or transport, schools or sanitary posts, expelling peasants from the land, police brutality, political manipulation, unemployment, government indifference, authorities' corruption, and personal and family problems. Bible and life are not separated but are considered the two "books" from God. Both are read. People read their lives with the eyes of the Bible, and they read the Bible with the eyes of their lives. They can see themselves in the Bible, in the persons and events of the people of God; they can discover the liberating power of God through history, both in the past and in the present. And they can hold onto the promise and the vision of the kingdom and the challenge to search for justice, love, freedom, and dignity according to God's purpose.

They do not separate evangelization from social action—maybe most of them do not know the difference, not being used to our neat definitions and dichotomies. But they can understand that what God promises and God demands is to be done. Theirs really is a discipleship in the kingdom.

Evangelization in this kingdom perspective is natural and effective. It is not only verbal proclamation, but also the incarnation of the gospel in the lives of the people and the community. The

Catholic bishops (who did not invent or promote these Base Christian Communities) when they met in Medellín in 1968, had to
recognize the evangelistic potential of this movement, saying in one
of their pastoral documents: "The basic Christian community is the
first and fundamental ecclesial nucleus . . . the initial cell of the
ecclesial structures, and the *focus of evangelization,* and it currently
serves as the most important source of human advancement and
development."[17]

Evangelization and human development go together! Most of the
people participating in the Base Christian Communities were already nominal Christians, baptized Christians, but now they had
become disciples! This is not numerical church growth (all of them
were considered members of the church) but it is evangelization—
making the gospel real and effective in their lives and their community. This is evangelization *within* the church! Even more, it is
becoming the evangelization *of* the church, challenging the traditional church and its hierarchy to new understandings of the gospel!
For the Latin American church the great discovery of this century
has been that "not only the Church is evangelizing the poor but the
poor are evangelizing the Church!" Consequently, the church can
reach a new authenticity, a new credibility, to proclaim the good
news of the kingdom to those outside. Only God knows the impact
on the nonbelievers, agnostics, and people of anti-Christian ideologies of a church that is able to present a new face and new life. A
church that is not living for itself but, like the Master, for others, for
the kingdom.

COSTLY DISCIPLESHIP

Bonhoeffer spoke of "costly discipleship" in his classic exposition
of the Sermon on the Mount. In time—as a prisoner of Hitler, and
finally executed by a firing squad—he would know by personal
experience how costly it might become to be a consistent disciple in
this world. Many Christians in Latin America today (as in other parts
of the world) are discovering the meaning of discipleship in the
kingdom—and paying the price for it.

As Jesus said, the kingdom "makes violence" and "suffers violence." He told his disciples in advance that he was sending them
"as sheep in the midst of wolves" (Matt. 10:16). They should have no

illusions. They have hated him and rejected him. The disciples should not expect different treatment: "a disciple is not above his teacher" (Matt. 10:24; Luke 6:40); "if they persecuted me, they will persecute you too; if they obeyed my teaching, they will obey yours too" (John 15:20, TEV). Discipleship in the kingdom takes place in the world where the forces of the antikingdom are operating.

Before the kingdom, we have to make a choice: for or against it; with the kingdom or with the antikingdom; with life or with the antilife; for Christ or against him: "Anyone who is not for me is really against me; anyone who does not help me gather is really scattering" (Matt. 12:30).

One of the most difficult challenges for Christians today is to test the spirits, to read the signs of the times, to see clearly where the line of division between the kingdom and the antikingdom is today. In Bonhoeffer's times the Confessing church in Germany came to this division and confronted Nazism, while many others were silent or cooperating with it. In today's Latin America, many Christians have found in the defense of human rights, this line of division and confession.[18] In the Pre–Melbourne Consultation, held in Peru, immediately after the Evangelism Conference (CLADE II), a group of Christians put it this way:

How do we discern the signs of the Kingdom?

There, where a just order is sought; there, where human life is respected and a full life is fostered; there, where women and men live in solidarity; there, where the structures of society try to favor "the orphan, the widow and the poor"; there, where human beings have the opportunity to become what God intends them to be; THERE, the Kingdom of God is at work.

On the contrary, there, where the social system is bound to favor a few in detriment of the majority of the members of society; there, where injustice divides and puts people against people; there, where dictatorial regimes curtail freedom and tread under foot the fundamental rights of people; THERE, the anti-kingdom is at work.[19]

Father Rutilio Grande of El Salvador was one who made his choice as a disciple in the kingdom and identified the forces of the antikingdom. In a country like El Salvador, where fourteen families own most of the land, with an overcrowded and poor population, and 40 percent of children die of malnutrition before age five, it was not difficult to see where the forces of antilife were operating. This is how a fellow Jesuit describes what Father Rutilio did:

> With great attachment to and respect for the *campesinos*, and concern for the practice of religion, Rutilio pursued his purpose: "We want to build up with you communities of brothers and sisters, without the division of oppressor and oppressed, which will allow all of us to build up a more just society, such as corresponds to the plans of God." The gospel was the moving force on the way to that goal. After only half a year, forty local communities had been formed, with their own "animators," courses, celebrations. They were discovering themselves as human beings, as brothers and sons, sisters and daughters of God. Within the first year they could see, in a strike of more than two thousand landworkers at the most important refinery in the area, the sustained effort of the workers in the struggles to have their rights assured to them.

> The inhuman condition led the *campesinos* to read the gospel with new eyes, and the good news shed new light on their situation: it led to a critique that went to the root of the evil.

> Rutilio defended the right of the poor to organize themselves. Soon the rumor started going around that he was an agitator, a subversive—yes, a Communist.[20]

This is an old game: to give names. They called Jesus subversive—and executed him. This is the risk of any disciple who tries to give names to the powers, to the oppressors, to the demons. He or she can make mistakes—and they can be named and eliminated. Jesus they called "Beelzebub"; the many Christians who dare to live among the poor and oppressed or to render their voice for them may be called subversive or Communist.

On February 13, 1977, Father Rutilio Grande preached a sermon, where he said: "I am very disturbed, my brothers and sisters, my friends, that soon the Bible will not be allowed to cross the border into El Salvador. If Christ were to come to El Salvador (the land of the Savior), he would be crucified all over again."[21]

Less than a month after his public statement, as he was on his way home, he and the *campesinos* Manuel and Nelson were shot down by machine guns. " 'I am going to where God's love is!' were his last words before the machine-gun blast, reported to us by one of the three children with him who miraculously survived the attack."[22]

Father Rutilio's understanding of the kingdom gospel is reflected in one of the songs his community sang: "We will follow in faith the man from Nazareth. We will take part in his work, to help the justice of the kingdom of God break through. Jesus of Nazareth is the advent of the kingdom of the Father."[23]

Father Rutilio was buried beside his two *campesino* friends, sealed with the baptism of martyrdom, under the floor in front of the altar of the church in El Paismal where he was born. One of the *campesinos* had been baptized in that same place by Father Rutilio fifteen years earlier.

It was Rutilio's sense of discipleship in the kingdom, in a situation of great suffering and polarization, that led him to take sides. His friends and colleagues in the ministry have called him "Martyr for the Evangelization of El Salvador." For them, "Rutilio Grande, ever since his martyr death, has become a symbol and banner for a people that suffers and struggles to free itself, for a church that dies and rises again, for the Jesuits who go to those on the margin of society, who champion the cause of justice, in the discipleship of Christ, the man from Nazareth."[24]

Costly discipleship—and powerful evangelization in the kingdom perspective—the power of the grain that has to die in order for the plant to grow and produce (John 12:24).

CONVERSION TO THE KINGDOM AND IN THE KINGDOM

As we have seen in Jesus' evangelization of the in-breaking kingdom, the challenge of the kingdom issues a call to conversion. And, as Jim Wallis rightly says, "conversion in the New Testament can only be understood from the perspective of the Kingdom of God. . . . To be converted to Christ meant to give one's allegiance to the Kingdom."

This is something that we really need to recover in our present evangelization where conversion is focused on a purely personal (and individualistic and privatistic) transaction between the soul and God. Certainly, conversion is a very personalizing experience—we come face to face with God and make the most eventful decision of our life. Jesus made his call to conversion in a very personalized way: "Follow me." Jesus always began his call to discipleship by looking at the person—Levi at the tax collector's counter, Zacchaeus in the tree, Nathanael under the tree—and loving that person, for example, the Young Ruler.

Jesus' call was to turn to *God* and his *kingdom*, present in *him*. It was an invitation to enter into a community and into a movement. Jesus' call is personal but not individualistic or privatistic. To turn to *Christ* is to *turn to the kingdom*, to turn to *others*. Jesus asked the Rich Young Ruler to go "to the poor" and then to come and "follow me." Zacchaeus was declared inside salvation and inside the community of the kingdom ("son of Abraham") because he was ready to put his economic and social relationships in line with the kingdom. In the New Testament there is no "hot line" to God that is not connected through the neighbor. To love God and the neighbor are the first and second commandments (Matt. 22:37–40). You cannot love God if you do not love your brother; to love our brothers and sisters is to pass from death to life (1 John 4:7–8, 20; 3:17–18). And the reverse is true also: "We love because he first loved us," the "new commandment: love one another . . . as I have loved you" (1 John 4:19; 4:10; 3:16; John 13:34; 15:12–17). There can be no vertical reconciliation with God (offering at the altar) unless you make horizontal reconciliation with your brother who may have something against you (Matt. 5:24). Nor can you be forgiven sins by the Father if you do not forgive those who sin against you (Matt. 6:12, 14–15; 18:21–35). To receive a "little one" is to receive Christ himself, and to serve "one of the least of these" is the only way to serve the king before inheriting the eternal kingdom (Matt. 18:1–3; 25:31–46). This is what Yves Congar has called "the Sacrament of the neighbor"!

Conversion to Christ means conversion to the neighbor. Conversion to Christ—in the neighbor. We need to incorporate this in our call to conversion, if we want to be faithful to the gospel of the kingdom and to the total witness of the Scriptures in our evangelization.

Gustavo Gutiérrez, the well-known Latin American liberation theologian, tells us that this conversion has been a long process for the present generation of Christians in Latin America. They were at first "unaware" and "unconcerned" about the situation of the people, and made a radical separation between the religious and the secular, this life and the next. Then they began to be "aware" of the suffering and the problems of the people and tried to develop helping programs by applying some social principles from the church. They moved into politics to try to change the situation through legislation. Gradually, through more rigorous analysis of poverty and exploitation and their sources in international and national structures, these Christians became "radicalized." They made "the major discovery of our generation": the discovery of the "other"—the neighbor. And this was a true conversion experience. As Gutiérrez describes it:

> To follow the itinerary which we have recalled in its main milestones, meant to many Christians the possibility of taking a further step and to enter gradually into a new world of the other. The world of the poor, of the oppressed, of the exploited classes.
>
> Love of neighbor is an essential component of Christian existence. But while I consider my neighbor, the "near" one, the one I find on my way, the one who comes to me asking for help, my world remains the same. . . . If, on the contrary, I consider my neighbor the one to whom I move . . . the "far away" neighbor, in the streets, in farms, factories and mines, then my world changes.
>
> The poor is for the gospel the neighbor par excellence. The option for the poor has become the axle around which revolves a new way of being human and being Christian in Latin America. Actually, we are before a true process of evangelical conversion, namely, the getting out of oneself and the opening to God and others. This is a process that a growing number of Christians are passing through in Latin America. Conversion not so much as an intimate attitude, privatist and idealist, but in a socially conditioned environment of human, cultural, socio-economic and political realities which have to be transformed.
>
> In fact, the liberating engagement is coming to mean for many Christians an authentic spiritual experience. . . . The poor, the other, emerges as the revealer of the Wholly Other. [25]

In reading these descriptions of a generational experience of conversion we come to a paradox. When we speak of conversion, particularly in the context of evangelization, we speak of the conversion of the unbelievers or of those coming from other religions and beliefs. But here the Peruvian theologian is speaking of the conversion of Christians! This is a surprise on the way of the kingdom, of which Jesus himself gave many hints. The fascinating thing about *conversion in the kingdom* is that, even though it has a first moment of turning, of radical decision, of new beginning, it is also an ongoing process. The conversion of the evangelizer continues in the process of evangelizing! Is it not true that we grow in understanding of the gospel the more we share it and learn from those with whom we want to share it?

That, precisely, was Peter's experience. When we speak of conversion, we think of Paul's unique experience or somebody like the jailer from Philippi. We seldom go to Peter for a conversion sermon. The reason may be that we do not know when he was converted: he had so many conversions! The first one was his entrance into discipleship through his brother Andrew (John 1:40–42). The second conversion was his awareness of being a sinful person in the presence of Jesus' authority and power (Luke 5:1–11). Then he came to his third conversion when he was illuminated to confess Jesus as Christ, the Son of the Living God, and to make profession of faith before the others (Mark 8:27–30). After his shameful negation of Jesus, he was rehabilitated and reinstated by the resurrected Lord as a shepherd of the sheep, through his triple affirmation of love for Jesus Christ (John 21:15–19). Then he had what might be considered a fifth conversion during his experience of the Holy Spirit in Pentecost (Acts 2:4, 36–38). And even the Pentecostal experience was not enough! The story of his visions and the call to go to Cornelius's house marks another of his spiritual crises of conversion and growth. This time he had a theological block: his separation of clean and unclean food, his attitude toward the Gentile world. He needed three visions and a visit to persuade him to go to Cornelius's house. Then and there he saw how the Spirit of God was already working among the non-Jews: "I now see how true it is that God has no favourites" (Acts 10:34, NEB).

This is the exciting thing about conversion in the kingdom and discipleship evangelization: we are on the way, following Jesus, witnessing to the kingdom in every imaginable situation, in a process of constant conversion, until the day when the kingdom will come in its fullness and "God will be all in all."

End of the Eclipse?

This exploration has been longer and more difficult than I had anticipated. There were moments and periods of "eclipse" in my own search for visions, hints, and directions for evangelization in the perspective of the kingdom. But I had the strong feeling that, even in the shadow cone, the Lord was pushing me toward the coming light. Obviously, the task of developing an adequate biblical foundation and a systematic theological formulation for kingdom evangelization is beyond my resources and abilities. I am more conscious than ever of my limitations for this task. There will be many others more capable of continuing with it. But I am also firmly convinced that this is the right direction, and that we are going to get out of the eclipse.

One thing is absolutely clear: we need to claim and to recover the totality of the biblical gospel for our evangelization. Which means, first of all, that we need to recover the original message of Jesus on the reign of God and the kingdom perspective for our motivation and strategy. We have to integrate Jesus' message in the Gospels with the totality of the New Testament witness in our theology for evangelization and in our evangelistic message. A purely Pauline theology—mediated through the Reformation and narrowed by some of our historical or sectarian reformulations—will not do it. A watered-down gospel of the "teachings" of the "historical Jesus" on "God's Fatherhood and human brotherhood" will not do it either, much less a gospel encapsulated in the missiles of contemporary apocalypticism.

By contrast, it is obvious that our traditional minitheologies of evangelization (the "plan of salvation," or "four spiritual laws" type

115

of kerygmatic reduction) do not do justice to the whole gospel, and they cannot match the desperate needs of the people or the challenges of our troubled world.

We live in a world on the brink of nuclear annihilation with millions starving to death or living subhuman lives in the midst of abundant resources accessible only to a few. The most advanced societies are caught in the idolatries of modern materialism and consumerism, or submerged in the underworld of drug addiction, crime, and esoteric cults. This is a world of untold suffering and oppression, frustrated revolutions, incredible violations of human rights, unbelievable refinements of torture, or rampant genocide. Millions of children are condemned to die of malnutrition before their first or their fifth year of life, or to suffer brain damage for the rest of their lives, such as they are. This world has enormous resources and faces great and challenging tasks—forming new generations, raising human life to the status of God's revealed purpose, building new societies, and incarnating God's love in fraternal and caring communities. In such a world, it will not be enough to go around the globe "saving souls" with a census chart to get individuals to make "instant decisions" for Christ.

We need to recover the capacity to dream. The reign of God is God's own dream, his project for his world and for humanity! He made us dreamers, and he wants us to be seduced by his dream and to dream with him. We might say, paraphrasing J. H. Forest, that "It is not we who dream but God who dreams in us." Only a God-inspired and God-sustained hope will free us from despair and cynicism in the face of so much sin and ugliness. As Henri Nouwen says in his book *Clowning in Rome:*

> It is a world clouded with an all-pervading fear, a growing sense of despair, and the paralyzing awareness that humanity has come to the verge of suicide. We no longer have to ask ourselves if we are approaching a state of emergency. We are in the midst of it here and now.

Responding to this, Forest rightly reflects:

> But alarm clocks are useful for only a few moments; they are not meant to ring throughout the day. When fear becomes a constant howling, instead of awakening us, it paralyzes and deadens us. . . . The expectation of unparalleled catastrophe can take root in us in such a way that what we dread becomes more certain in our psychological and spiritual

surrender to fear. It is fear that constantly animates arms race and fuels lusts for power . . . and so often imprisons our response.[1]

Much preaching is also inspired by fear and manipulates with fear. But God has promised us that "your young [people] shall see visions, and your old [people] shall dream dreams" (Acts 2:17). And that is what the Holy Spirit was sent for! Let us then dream together with prophets, poets, apocalypticists, and apostles. The proclamation of the kingdom in the power of the Spirit can enlarge our horizons, raise our hopes, and make us dream again. Nothing is more urgent in our world today to both the restless peoples of the Third World and the fearful peoples of the First and Second Worlds.

We need to recover, with the totality of the gospel of the kingdom, the prophetic evangelization of the Bible tradition. The annunciation of the kingdom of God demands the denunciation of the kingdoms of men and of powers, which are destroying human life and exploiting creation. And we need to name the idols. "The spiritual powers in the air" are also concrete and visible as the economic, financial, industrial, technological, political, cultural, and military powers of "this dark world." We need to be constantly reminded that "our fight is not against human foes, but against . . . powers" (Eph. 6:12, NEB). Our evangelization falls short of the mark if we limit ourselves to naming the personal sins and commending the personal virtues without pointing to collective sins, structural powers, and societal trends. This is what a kingdom perspective can do for us.

But, at the same time, we need to keep the personal and pastoral dimensions of the gospel. Evangelization has to become real and be incarnated in persons and human relationships. To share the gospel means to minister to persons in their needs and in their particular situations. To announce the gospel of Christ means to share in Jesus' concern for persons and his compassion for the crowd, for "the scattered masses," for the "little ones," and "the least of these." One of the most promising insights we have seen in our exploration is Raymond Fung's idea of the "sinned-against." We need to look at people in the Spirit of Jesus, not only as "sinners" but as "sinned-against," especially the poor and oppressed. This is also part of our Christian heritage, particularly the original compassion movements inspired by the evangelical revivals, as David O. Moberg has shown in *The Great Reversal: Evangelism Versus Social Concern*.[2]

We also need to recover the communal dimension of the church—and of evangelization. The Base Christian Communities may well be a gift from God to our generation to remind us that the kingdom takes shape in a partial and proleptic way in small committed communities of the faithful. Protestants, particularly those belonging to mainline churches, need to remember that we come from the *collegia pietatis*, the "religious societies," and the *ecclesioa in ecclesia*. The discovery in the Base Christian Communities of personhood, human solidarity, and hope for society is not solely for Third World peoples. That experience is essential for those in industrial societies, as well—where millions are starving for genuine community life, languishing in loneliness, fear, and alienation, and clinging to the poor substitutes of television and the "electronic church" with its computerized "personal letters" and appeals for money.

It is also obvious that church growth per se cannot be taken as the whole of Christian mission or the overpowering motivation for evangelization. We are not sent to preach the church but to announce the kingdom. Nobody is more aware of the need for quality growth, together with quantity growth, than some of those engaged in the "church growth movement" who speak of "organic growth" (Alan Tippett) and "prophetic growth" (Orlando Costas). Here is where we need to combine evangelization with discipleship in the kingdom and for the kingdom—intentional discipleship, militant discipleship. Church growth is still possible in the traditional "Christian" lands, and necessary in areas of the "non-Christian" world. But to send cross-cultural missionaries from the former to the latter will not be enough. The fact that some of the greatest threats for the future of humanity and some of the most distressing moral crises of our time are taking place in the so-called Christian West should be a sobering thought. The two nuclear superpowers belong to a tradition of centuries and millenniums of exposure to Christianity, formed by a Christian ethos. The nation that is sending more missionaries to the rest of the world is also the only nation that has ever dropped an atomic bomb. That bomb was made, carried, and dropped by Christians. The intercontinental missiles are aimed at, among others, Christians meeting in churches in Eastern Europe or America. We need to hear Stanley Jones's plea to the churches in relation to announcing the kingdom:

In the World Conference on Missions in 1938, a time when fascism, naziism, and communism were rising to ascendancy and when the ecumenical movement was rising amid the Christian churches, the thought of the missionary conference in Madras began flowing toward the ecumenical church as the answer to those earthborn totalitarianisms. I pleaded that we make the kingdom of God our stand and thus match against these earthborn relativisms God's absolute—the Kingdom. They preferred to make ecumenical church their stand—to match against relativisms another relativism, the ecumenical church. "Suppose," I said, "you go out and cry, 'Repent for the ecumenical church is at hand' "; what would be the reaction? The people would laugh at you, as they laugh when I suggest it to audiences. But you don't laugh when I say, "Repent for the kingdom of God is at hand"; that is, if you have any sense, you don't laugh, you bend the knee.[3]

Unfortunately, there are many who do not have "any sense" and may not "bend the knee" before a proclamation of an absolute kingdom. But it is equally true that no proclamation of kingdom will make sense for the world if the kingdom with all its implications is not taken seriously by Christians themselves. There is no genuine evangelization (toward the inside of the church and toward those outside it) without kingdom discipleship. It is not only a matter of *credibility* but of *authenticity* and *faithfulness* to the gospel.

In the kingdom perspective there are a great variety of tasks to be performed, and there is room for all Christians and all churches. There is room for special vocations and gifts in the evangelistic task, and in the total witness of the churches. There is room as well for different styles, emphases, and missiological ideologies—provided we share in the all-encompassing horizon of the kingdom. We can have all the variety in the world if we can press toward unity—the unity of vision, faith, and commitment in the kingdom. For unity is also part of the witness to the kingdom, one of the signs of the presence of the kingdom. Again, this is not only a matter of credibility ("that the world may believe"), it is also a matter of consistency with the gospel we proclaim.

Thank God that, with the enormity of the task, we have also great resources and assets: the Scriptures, with "the subversive memory of Jesus" and the totality of witness to the gospel of the kingdom; and the promise of the Holy Spirit: "you will receive power and you will be my witnesses," "the Spirit of Truth will make you remember all that I have told you . . . and he will lead you into all truth" (John 16:4–15).

I have loaded these chapters with quotations from the Scriptures and with bibliographical references. They do not pretend to be scholarly or even systematic, merely indicators of the richness of the Scriptures on the kingdom gospel and the usefulness of the insights drawn from a century of research in the area of the New Testament message. We need to do our homework as evangelists, teachers, and disciples in the churches. And we need theologians, seminaries, and publishing houses to make accessible and usable to the whole church the tremendous biblical and theological resources for an evangelization in the kingdom perspective.

There are enormous resources in the world church: The World Council of Churches—bringing together from the three worlds Christians and their human, theological, spiritual, material resources—and its commitment to holistic mission in the world. The fantastic renewal and vitality of the Roman Catholic church and its increasing worldwide influence on the causes of peace, reconciliation, justice, and freedom, together with its clear commitment to a creative and new understanding of evangelization. The tremendous thrust of evangelical missions with their concern for "reaching the unreached" and finishing the "unfinished task of the church" of the evangelization of the whole world. The amazing new missions originated and expanding in the Third World. The ever-renewing force of Christian workers and missionaries, research centers, new instruments of communications, and the like. And, last but not least, the power of intercession, the network of prayer and concern, surrounding the earth—vertical and horizontal intercession before God and before people and powers.

There are as well great and unique resources in the local churches. No movement or institution in the world can compare with the reality of millions gathering every week in local congregations around the world to pray, to celebrate, and to proclaim the reign of God. There is where a holistic announcement of the kingdom can take place as the natural projection of the local church in proclamation (kerygma), fellowship (koinonia), celebration (leiturgia), teaching and learning (didache), and service (diakonia).

Such proclamation would be rooted in the real life of the people and in the heart of the community.

The most encouraging sign is that the kingdom eclipse is passing. There is a converging and exciting trend toward recovering the totality of the Christian gospel in the kingdom of God perspective. The two subverters of history are strongly at work: the subversive memory of Jesus in the Scriptures and the subversive (antiamnesic) work of the Holy Spirit in the Christian community throughout history.

We are getting out of the shadow cone. We are beginning to see the shining edge of the sun, and soon we will again be in daylight.

For the darkness shall turn to dawning
and the dawning to noonday break
And Christ's great Kingdom shall come to earth
A Kingdom of love and light.[4]

Notes

Introduction

1. Mortimer Arias, ed., *Evangelización y Revolución en América Latina* (Montevideo: Iglesia Metodista, 1969).

2. Mortimer Arias, "Bolivian Manifesto on Evangelization in Latin America Today," *Monthly Letter About Evangelism* (Geneva: WCC Commission on World Mission and Evangelism, February 1975).

3. Mortimer Arias, "That the World May Believe," *International Review of Mission* (January 1976), 21ff. Also published in G. H. Anderson and Thomas F. Stransky, eds., *Mission Trends No. 3: Theologies from the Third World* (New York: Paulist Press; Grand Rapids: Wm. B. Eerdmans, 1976), 84–103.

4. Mortimer Arias, *Venga tu Reino: La Memoria Subversiva de Jesus* (Mexico: Casa Unida de Publicaciones, 1980).

5. See report on the workshop by the Evangelism Secretary of the Commission on World Mission and Evangelism, John Kurewa, in *Monthly Letter About Evangelism* (Geneva: WCC, July 1976), and his mimeo, "Report of the Workshop on Evangelism," June 4–15, 1979.

6. Seminars were held at the Overseas Missionary Study Center, in Ventnor, New Jersey; at Port Moresby, New Guinea, under the auspices of the South Pacific Conference of Churches; and at the Seminario Biblico Latinoamericano in San José, Costa Rica, during the months of April, May, and June 1980.

7. A notable exception was E. Stanley Jones, the famous missionary to India and world evangelist who gladly acknowledged he was "obsessed" with the kingdom of God, and who consistently tried for half a century to present the gospel in that perspective, relating it to the quest of modern man and the problems of society and using his experiences in India and his reading of science, particularly psychology. But, then, why was he ignored by those more concerned with evangelization? Was it because of his "liberal" mind-set or because of the lack of awareness of the centrality of the kingdom in the biblical message and in Jesus' own gospel? For a recent evaluation of his missiological contribution, see "The Legacy of E. Stanley

Jones," *International Bulletin of Missionary Research* (1982). A typical
summary of his own position is E. Stanley Jones, *The Unshakeable Kingdom
and the Unchanging Person* (Nashville: Abingdon Press, 1972).

C. Peter Wagner, Professor of Church Growth at Fuller Theological
Seminary and prolific author on this movement, has an interesting suggestion about this question, coming from his personal experience and from
his intimate knowledge of the conservative evangelical churches in the
United States and abroad. He candidly confesses that he has never
preached a sermon on the kingdom of God, and he does not recollect
hearing a sermon on the subject. Trying to respond to the question "where
has the kingdom been" for the evangelicals all these years, he begins by
telling us that in 1950, when he became a Christian, he identified himself
with the Inter-Varsity Christian Fellowship, which at the time was "engaged
in a serious theological warfare . . . against liberalism, against post-millen-
nialism, against evolution, against Freudian psychology, against naturalism,
against humanism—all of which could be more or less summed up in the
term 'the social gospel.'" Wagner believes that since Walter Rauschen-
busch, "the principal advocate" of the social gospel, had "used the kingdom
of God motif as the major integrating element of his theological development," this made it unpalatable to evangelical minds and ears. He concludes: "By association, then, the kingdom of God became an enemy of
evangelicals. Feelings were so strong that some went to the extreme of
opposing any sort of Christian activity designed to heal the hurts of society."
Wagner also blames dispensationalism and the second-coming charts, which
put the kingdom totally in the future with little bearing on life today, as
another misuse of the kingdom of God idea. The result has been that
"evangelicals during most of the twentieth century chose to concentrate
largely on soul saving." Wagner is optimistic, however, about the future. He
affirms: "Evangelicals may have buried the kingdom of God concept, but
they never buried the Bible. . . . Because it is biblical, evangelicals are
prone to listen." Let us hope that both "evangelicals" and "mainliners" may
listen to the biblical record on the kingdom of God, for the sake of the
gospel, for the sake of the church, and for the sake of the evangelization of
the world. Eight decades of this century handicapped by the antikingdom
problem in a substantial sector of the Christian church is too long a time.
The recovery of the kingdom perspective for evangelization is largely over-
due! See C. Peter Wagner, *Church Growth and the Whole Gospel: A
Biblical Mandate* (New York: Harper & Row, 1981), 2–4.

8. The following works include a historical and critical review of more
than eight decades of scholarship on the teachings of Jesus, focusing on the
kingdom of God. Norman Perrin, *The Kingdom of God in the Teaching of
Jesus* (Philadelphia: Westminster Press, 1963); George Eldon Ladd, *Jesus
and the Kingdom: The Eschatology of Biblical Realism* (New York: Harper &
Row, 1964); Herman N. Ridderbos, *The Coming of the Kingdom* (Philadel-

phia: Presbyterian and Reformed Publishing Co., 1962). Georgia Harkness has made a useful summary of the main trends in the interpretation of the kingdom of God in her *Understanding the Kingdom of God* (Nashville: Abingdon Press, 1974).

9. The most influential contemporary work on eschatology was Jürgen Moltmann's *Theology of Hope* (New York: Harper & Row, 1967). Wolfhart Pannenberg, another German theologian, has developed his eschatological concept of "the power of the future" in *Theology and the Kingdom of God* (Philadelphia: Westminster Press, 1969). Ewart H. Cousins has edited the presentations and discussions of the "Conference on Hope and the Future of Man" that brought together theologians from Europe and the United States in New York City, October 8–10, 1971: *Hope and the Future of Man* (Philadelphia: Fortress Press, 1972). On traditional eschatology and dispensationalism see L. Berkhof, *Systematic Theology* (Grand Rapids: Wm. B. Eerdmans, 1978). See also chap. 4, n. 2.

10. Oscar Cullman was one of the first contemporary scholars to relate mission to eschatology in his article "Eschatology and Mission in the New Testament," in *The Background of the New Testament and Its Eschatology*, ed. W. D. Davies and D. Daube (New York: Cambridge University Press, 1956), 409–21. The first systematic effort to base a theology of mission on eschatology is the stimulating book by Carl E. Braaten, *The Flaming Center: A Theology of Christian Mission* (Philadelphia: Fortress Press, 1977). Two leading missiologists, one from Europe and the other from South Africa, have taken the kingdom of God as the frame of reference to the understanding of Christian mission in recent works. See J. Verkuyl, *Contemporary Missiology: An Introduction* (Grand Rapids: Wm. B. Eerdmans, 1978), and David J. Bosch, *Witness to the World: The Christian Mission in Theological Perspective* (Atlanta: John Knox Press, 1980).

11. I am referring to the type of discipleship reflected in *Sojourners* and *The Other Side* magazines. The recent book by Jim Wallis, *The Call to Conversion: Recovering the Gospel for These Times* (New York: Harper & Row, 1981), is an excellent example of this new perspective of discipleship in the kingdom.

12. See books by George Eldon Ladd and Herman N. Ridderbos in n. 8. See also Howard A. Snyder, *The Community of the King* (Downers Grove, Ill.: Inter-Varsity Press, 1977).

13. C. Peter Wagner's effort to respond to the criticism that the Church Growth Movement has left out the kingdom of God in its theological foundations, however, seems to fall short of the challenge. Wagner goes a long way beyond current fundamentalism and evangelical individualism in his interpretation of kingdom of God style of life and implications for mission. Indeed he has some original and intriguing suggestions about the "signs of the kingdom" in Christian mission. And yet the impression is that the author has harnessed the kingdom of God theme to his Church Growth

chart rather than reappraising and putting Church Growth ideology under the judgment of the kingdom perspective. We must admire his courage and candor when he admits his former omissions: "I admit that I read the Scriptures with Church Growth eyes and . . . for years I filtered out the kingdom of God theme." With the same candor we ask: Is it possible that Wagner still looks at the kingdom theme with "Church Growth eyes," filtering out what does not fit into his assumed ecclesiology and his dualistic frame of theology? See Wagner, *Church Growth*, 4–19. Two recent evangelical works that are pointing in the direction of a kingdom perspective in evangelization are: Alfred C. Krass, *Five Lanterns at Sundown: Evangelism in a Chastened Mood* (Grand Rapids: Wm. B. Eerdmans, 1978), and Waldron Scott, *Bring Forth Justice: A Contemporary Perspective on Mission* (Grand Rapids: Wm. B. Eerdmans, 1980).

14. See Sergio Torres and John Eagleson, eds., *The Challenge of Basic Christian Communities* (Maryknoll, N.Y.: Orbis Books, 1980).

15. A. Altmann, Nelida Ritchie, and Hugo Zorrilla, *Jesucristo Vocación Compromotida con el Reino* (San José, Costa Rica: Consejo Latinoamericano de Iglesias [CLAI], 1982).

Chapter 1

1. I have discussed the origin and use of "evangelism" and "evangelization" in my Fondren Lectures (1977). See *Perkins Journal* (Winter 1979): 11–17.

2. See articles on *evangelion, evangelizestai, evangelizomai,* and *evangelistes* in G. Kittel and G. Friedrich, eds., *Theological Dictionary of the New Testament* (Grand Rapids: Wm. B. Eerdmans, 1964), 2: 706–25. [Ten vols., 1964–76, hereafter cited as *TDNT*.]

3. With the writing of the earliest canonical Gospels, "Gospels" became a new literary genre, with the purpose of telling the story of Jesus. But the word "gospel" was not used as a title for a book until A.D. 150. Cf. Willi Marxsen, *Mark the Evangelist* (Nashville: Abingdon Press, 1969), 117–50; Eduard Schweizer, *The Gospel According to Mark* (Atlanta: John Knox Press, 1977), 30, 44.

4. Paul VI, *Evangelii Nuntiandi*, Apostolic Exhortation on "Evangelization in the World Today," *Observatore Romano* (December 8, 1975). American translations in *The Pope Speaks*, 21, 1 (1976), 4–51; special editions in *Crux of the News* (Albany, N.Y.: Clarity Publishing, Inc., January 19, 1976), and in booklet form by the office of the American Conference of Bishops, Washington, D.C., nos. 7–8.

5. Eduard R. Dayton and David A. Fraser, *Planning Strategies for World Evangelization* (Grand Rapids: Wm. B. Eerdmans, 1980).

6. William R. Farmer has seriously challenged the accepted assumption among many scholars that Mark is the first written Gospel. See his recent discussions of the issue in his *Jesus and the Gospel: Tradition, Scripture, and Canon* (Philadelphia: Fortress Press, 1982), 1–11.

7. Werner H. Kelber has presented an exciting interpretation of Mark in terms of Jesus' proclamation of the kingdom in his *The Kingdom in Mark: A New Place and a New Time* (Philadelphia: Fortress Press, 1974). A detailed study of the kingdom message in Mark was done by A. M. Ambrozic, *The Hidden Kingdom: A Redactional-Critical Study of the References to the Kingdom of God in Mark's Gospel*, The Catholic Biblical Quarterly—Monograph Series, No. 2 (Washington, D.C.: Catholic Biblical Association of America, 1972). Agustin del Agua Perez, in his doctoral dissertation for the Universidad Pontificia de Comillas, Spain, made a similar study on Luke-Acts: *Evangelizar el Reino de Dios: Estudio Redaccional del Concepto Lucano de Basileia*, 1979. A summary of the main thesis has been published in *Estudios Biblicos* 38 (1979–80).

8. See Edward Schillebeeckx, *Jesus: An Experiment in Christology* (New York: Seabury Press, 1979), 107–13, for a useful discussion on the use of the word "gospel" in Mark, Matthew, Luke, and Paul.

9. Alan Walker, the Australian evangelist, has insisted on this holistic perspective, which includes the personal and the social, since his *The Whole Gospel for the Whole World* (New York: Abingdon Press, 1957). For a recent restatement of this perspective see Alan Walker, *The New Evangelism* (Nashville: Abingdon Press, 1975). Waldron Scott, former general secretary of the World Fellowship of Evangelicals, has made a strong case against common dichotomies among conservative evangelicals and has tried to formulate a holistic vision of mission from the perspective of the Scriptures in his *Bring Forth Justice* (Grand Rapids: Wm. B. Eerdmans, 1980). For the contemporary development of a more holistic view of the gospel and, consequently, of mission and evangelism, the indispensable reference book is Rodger C. Bassham's dissertation *Mission Theology, 1948–1975: Years of Worldwide Creative Tension—Ecumenical, Evangelical, and Roman Catholic* (Pasadena: William Carey, 1980).

10. Luke's prologue in the book of Acts describes the story of Jesus in terms of what "he *did* and *taught*" (Acts 1:1, italics added). Cf. the Melbourne Conference affirmation in the Report of Section III on "The Church Witness to the Kingdom": "The proclamation demands communication in deed and word, in teaching, learning and serving . . . word accompanies deed as the kingdom throws light ahead of its arrival and men and women seek to live in that light." *Your Kingdom Come* (Geneva: WCC, 1980), 195, 193.

11. Two Christian ethicists have dealt with the theme of the Jubilee in recent times: Etienne Trocmé, *Jesus Christ et la Revolution non-Violente* (Geneva: Labor et Fides, 1961), and John H. Yoder, expanding on the former, *The Politics of Jesus* (Grand Rapids: Wm. B. Eerdmans, 1972). Bishop Paulo Gregorious from the Mar-Thoma Church of India has written a provocative chapter on "To Proclaim Liberation, A Biblical Meditation on the Jubilee Year" in Richard D. N. Dickinson, *Set at Liberty the Oppressed*

(Geneva: WCC, 1975), 186–93. A recent systematic effort to deal with the Jubilee proclamation from a biblical perspective is the Ph. D. dissertation by Sharon H. Ringe, "The Jubilee Proclamation in the Ministry and Teaching of Jesus: A Tradition Critical Study in the Synoptic Gospels and Acts" (Union Theological Seminary, 1981, mimeographed). This comprehensive study, following the original insights from the work of James Sanders, shows that the Jubilee theme represents a common agenda for social justice and the liberation and transformation of human life throughout the Old Testament. It shows also that, according to Luke (4:18–19), Jesus presents himself as the evangelist (*mebasser*) of the new era of the kingdom, which incorporates all the themes and motifs of the Jubilee: personal and social, material and spiritual, historical and eschatological, associated with the content and context of Isa. 61:1–2. "Thus it might be said that for Luke, Jesus' identity and purpose are defined by Jubilee themes" (p. 156).

12. The concept of "apostle" (*apostolos*) is essentially being commissioned, being sent out with the purpose of proclamation of the kingdom (Luke 9:2; Matt. 10:5ff.). See *apostolos* in TDNT 2: 398–447; especially 424–30.

13. For the rich meaning of peace in the Old and New Testaments, which originated in the comprehensive concept of shalom, see biblical and theological dictionaries. J. C. Hoekendijk, the late and influential Dutch missiologist, proposed the concept of shalom as the most appropriate way to describe the content and meaning of the mission of God (*missio Dei*) and, consequently, the mission of the church. See his article, "The Call to Evangelism," *International Review of Mission* (Geneva: WCC, 1950): 41–55. This article has been reproduced in Donald McGavran, *Eye of the Storm* (Waco, Texas: Word Books, 1972), 219–30. Hoekendijk's ideas were further developed in *The Church Inside Out* (Philadelphia: Westminster Press, 1964), and in *Horizons of Hope* (Nashville: Tidings Publishing Co., 1970). See also the article on *eirene* in TDNT 2: 400–420.

14. The classic study on the words "kingdom," "kingdom of God," and "kingdom of heaven" in the Scriptures is the series of articles on *basileia* by K. L. Schmidt, H. Kleinknecht, K. G. Kuhn, and Gerhard von Rad in TDNT 3: 1–59. See also the article "Kingdom of God" by O. E. Evans in the *Interpreter's Dictionary of the Bible* (Nashville: Abingdon Press, 1962), 3: 24ff., probably the best short article on the subject. Other very valuable summary studies are B. Klappert, "King-Kingdom" in *The New International Dictionary of New Testament Theology*, ed. Colin Brown (Grand Rapids: Zondervan, 1977), 2: 372–90; Rudolf Schnackenburg, "Kingdom of God," in *Sacramentum Verbi: An Encyclopedia of Biblical Theology*, ed. Johannes B. Bauer (New York: Herder & Herder), 2: 455–70—see also his book, *God's Rule and the Kingdom* (New York: Herder & Herder, 1963); Stanley Brown and R. E. Brown, "The Kingdom of God," in *The Jerome*

Biblical Commentary (Englewood Cliffs, N.J.: Prentice-Hall, 1968), 2:782–84.

15. C. H. Dodd, *The Parables of the Kingdom*, rev. ed. (New York: Charles Scribner's Sons, 1961), 20. See also Joachim Jeremias, *The Parables of Jesus*, rev. ed., trans. S. H. Hooke (New York: Charles Scribner's Sons, 1963); idem, *Rediscovering the Parables*, trans. S. H. Hooke, adapted Frank Clarke (New York: Charles Scribner's Sons, 1966). Cf. John Dominic Crossan, *In Parables: The Challenge of the Historical Jesus* (New York: Harper & Row, 1973), 23–27.

16. Cf. Ernst Lohmeyer, *Our Father: An Introduction to the Lord's Prayer* (New York: Harper & Row, 1965), and Joachim Jeremias, *The Lord's Prayer* (Philadelphia: Fortress Press, 1964).

17. Günther Bornkamm, *Jesus of Nazareth*, trans. Irene McLuskey and Fraser McLuskey with James M. Robinson (New York: Harper & Row, 1960), 77. "All the beatitudes are directed towards the coming of the kingdom of God. . . ."

18. Norman Perrin, *Rediscovering the Teaching of Jesus* (New York: Harper & Row, 1967), 54.

Chapter 2

1. The poet William B. Yeats calls it "the Galilean turbulence" in "Two Songs from a Play," *Collected Poems* (New York, Macmillan Co., 1956), 210–11.

2. A standard work on the concept of the kingdom through the Old Testament is John Bright, *The Kingdom of God* (Nashville: Abingdon Press, 1953). See also Gerhard von Rad, "*Melek* and *malkuth* in the Old Testament," and Karl George Kuhn, "*Malkuth shamayim* in Rabbinic Literature," in *TDNT* 1: 565–74. On the origin of the idea of kingship in ancient Eastern religions, see John L. Mackenzie, "Aspects of Old Testament Thought: Relations Between God and Israel," *The Jerome Biblical Commentary* (Englewood Cliffs, N.J.: Prentice-Hall, 1968), 2:761, and the article on "The Kingdom of God," ibid., 2:782–84. For a very provocative interpretation of "Yahweh's kingdom" as "the seminal idea of the Old Testament," in its politico-religious implications, see George V. Pixley, *God's Kingdom: A Guide for Biblical Study*, trans. Donald D. Walsh (Maryknoll, N.Y.: Orbis Books, 1981).

3. Norman Perrin, *Rediscovering the Teachings of Jesus* (New York: Harper & Row, 1967), 63–67. On the meaning of "has come" or "has arrived" (from the Greek *ephthassen*), see C. H. Dodd, *The Parables of the Kingdom* (New York: Charles Scribner's Sons, 1961), 28 n. 1; W. G. Kümmel, *Promise and Fulfillment: The Eschatological Message of Jesus*, trans. Dorothea M. Barton (New York: Oxford University Press, 1957), 105–9.

4. *Entos hymōn* (see Kümmel, *Promise and Fulfillment*, 32–35; Jeremias, *New Testament Theology*, 101; Perrin, *Rediscovering*, 73–74, 55–56, may

be translated in Greek "within you" and "among you," but the latter is the
most accepted in the general context of Jesus' teachings.

   5. On the Greek word for "near" or "at hand" (engiken), see C. H. Dodd's
interpretation as "has arrived" or "has come" in Parables of the Kingdom,
27ff., and his fuller statement in the article, "The Kingdom of God Has
Come," in Expository Times 48 (1936–37): 138–41. A wider discussion of
interpretations appears in Kümmel, Promise and Fulfillment, 19–25. More
recently, Aloysius M. Abrozic, in his detailed The Hidden Kingdom: A
Redactional-Critical Study of the References to the Kingdom of God in
Mark's Gospel, The Catholic Biblical Quarterly—Monograph Series, No. 2
(Washington, D.C.: Catholic Association of America, 1972), reviews the old
discussion and, while realizing that the subject cannot be decided only by
philology, concludes that "it is commonly agreed that Mark 1:14–15 serves
as a programmatic statement which introduces, summarizes, and initiates
the ministry of Jesus" (p. 17). If we want to understand the meaning of near,
"one cannot eliminate the ministry [of Jesus] as one of the decisive events in
the total eschatological drama." As "a realized eschatological event" one has
to look at the ministry of Jesus. See also R. F. Berkey, "Eggizein, phthanein
and Realized Eschatology," Journal of Biblical Literature 82 (1963): 177–87.

   6. Herman Ridderbos, The Coming of the Kingdom (Phillipsburg, N.J.:
Presbyterian and Reformed Publishing Co., 1962), 70–76; G. E. Ladd,
Jesus and the Kingdom: The Eschatology of Biblical Realism (New York:
Harper & Row, 1964), 49, 160–62; Ambrozic, Hidden Kingdom, 25, 45.

   7. Dodd, Parables, 33–34; Jeremias, New Testament Theology, 108.

   8. Perrin, Rediscovering, 67.

   9. On "Who are the poor?" see Jeremias, New Testament Theology, 109.

   10. John Dominic Crossan has interpreted Jesus' parables as metaphors to
convey the inexpressible experience of the Wholly Other: "The Wholly
Other must always be radically new and one can experience it only within
its metaphors." The stories of the rabbis are didactic figures, those of Jesus
are poetic metaphors; theirs are subservient to the teaching situations;
those of Jesus are subservient only to the experienced revelation which
seeks to articulate its presence in, by, and through them." Crossan poses an
analogy between poetic and religious experiences (which in Jesus are mar-
velously combined) in that "in both cases the experience-as-gift and the
expression-in-metaphor are combined at the heart of the event." The presence of the kingdom in Jesus, then, is experience-as-gift, and it is expressed
in metaphors (parables). "This is what Jesus' parables seek to do: to help
others into their own experience of the Kingdom and to draw from that
experience their own way of life." In Parables: The Challenge of the Historical Jesus (New York: Harper & Row, 1973), 13, 20–21, 19, 52. Cf. the
esoteric comment of the evangelist: "Jesus preached his message to the
people, using many parables like these . . . and he could not speak to them
without using parables" (Mark 4:33–34).

11. Jürgen Moltmann, *The Trinity and the Kingdom* (New York: Harper & Row, 1981), 69–70.

12. Jesus' unique expression for God was "Abba," the colloquial word used in Aramean (Jesus' mother tongue) by a child for his or her father. This was the intimate way Jesus spoke to God in his prayers: "Father" (Abba). He taught his disciples to do the same. Here are some examples: "Father"— Mark 14:36; Luke 22:42; 23:34, 46; John 17:1, 11, 21, 24, 25 (all in the context of Jesus addressing God in prayer). "My Father"—Matt. 1:21; 10:32; 11:27; 12:50; 18:10; 24:36; Mark 14:36; Luke 2:49; 22:42; 23:34; John 2:16; 5:17, 43; 8:49; 12:26; 14:20; 15:1. "Your Father"—Matt. 5:48; 6:6, 15; 7:11; 18:14; Luke 6:36; 11:13; 12:32. "Our Father"—Matt. 6:9; Luke 11:2. "My Father and your Father"—John 20:17. See Jeremias, *New Testament Theology*, 61–68. Cf. also *The Central Message of the New Testament* (Philadelphia: Fortress Press, 1981).

13. Moltmann, *Trinity and the Kingdom*, 70.

14. *The Gospel of Thomas* 81:28—82:3, as quoted by Crossan, *In Parables*, 34–35. See Crossan's classification of parables of advent, reversal, and action, 57–58.

15. C. S. Lewis, *Surprised by Joy: The Shape of My Early Life* (New York: Harcourt, Brace & Co., 1956).

16. Jeremias, *New Testament Theology*, 113–21.

17. Hans Küng, *On Being a Christian*, trans. Edward Quinn (New York: Doubleday & Co., 1976), 273–76.

18. Jon Sobrino, *Christology at the Crossroads: A Latin American Approach* (Maryknoll, N.Y.: Orbis Books, 1978), 49.

19. Jesus' acts of healing were also acts of proclamation, signs of the presence and power of the kingdom. Jesus never used healing as a means of attraction or a demonstration of his divine power. That was the temptation he had rejected at the beginning of his ministry (Matt. 4:6–7; Luke 4:9–11). In the synoptic stories Jesus consistently put himself out of the picture, leaving the individual in the presence of God: "Your faith has made you whole." Jesus never invited people to bring their sick, but he always responded out of compassion for the people. It was a matter of faith producing healing and not healing producing faith. It is a remarkable fact that the Greek word for "miracle" (*thauma*) is never used in the Gospels. Jesus' acts of healing and exorcism are called "signs" (*semeia*) and mighty acts (*dynamis*) of the work (*erga*) of Jesus.

20. Küng, *On Being a Christian*, 273–76.

21. Juan Luis Segundo uses these passages to illustrate Jesus' hermeneutics, starting from life, over against the theological hermeneutics of the Pharisees, starting from their own ideologies. See *The Liberation of Theology* (Maryknoll, N.Y.: Orbis Books, 1976), 77ff.

22. Etienne Trocmé, *Jesus de Nazareth* (Neuchâtel: Delachaux et Niestlé, 1971), 101–10.

23. Sobrino, *Christology,* 101–10.

24. Ibid., 208. On this issue see also N. A. Dahl, "The Problem of the Historical Jesus," in *Kerygma and History,* ed. Carl Braaten and Roy Harrisville (Nashville: Abingdon Press, 1962); William R. Farmer, *Jesus and the Gospel* (Philadelphia: Fortress Press, 1982), 26ff., 40, 44; Perrin, *Rediscovering,* 102–3.

Chapter 3

1. "Already" and "not yet" have become popular expressions among New Testament scholars who have reached a certain consensus about the present and future dimensions of the kingdom of God in the teaching of Jesus. Oscar Cullmann in *Christ and Time: The Primitive Christian Conception of Time and History,* rev. ed. (Philadelphia: Westminster Press, 1964), gave unforgettable expression to this eschatological tension with his example from World War II, when the Allied forces decided on disembarkment day (D-Day) to counterattack the German forces in Europe, and planned for the final victory (V-Day) but without knowing its exact date. Since Jesus inaugurated the kingdom, we live between the D-Day and the V-Day, the present kingdom and the imminent kingdom. See Isaac C. Rottenberg, *The Promise and the Presence: Toward a Theology of the Kingdom of God* (Grand Rapids: Wm. B. Eerdmans, 1980), 43–54.

2. Eschatology, from the Greek *eschaton,* means last things, and it has been used to refer to that part of theology that deals with the "last things": the end of the world, the final judgment, heaven and hell, life eternal, the return of Christ, and the consummation of the kingdom. This has been also a sort of *last* chapter in theology (in some theologies it has become a *lost* chapter!), the exception being the sectarian Adventist movements and dispensationalist interpretations of the Scriptures with their exaggerated emphasis on the end of the world, the second coming, the Armageddon, the millennium, and the like. Eschatology has come strongly to its own with the help of Jürgen Moltmann and his book *Theology of Hope.* Moltmann, who believes that eschatology is not merely an appendix of theology but the golden thread (promise) of biblical theology, has remarked that "the discovery of eschatology for the message and existence of Jesus and for early Christianity . . . is undoubtedly one of the most important events in recent Protestant theology." *Theology of Hope* (New York: Harper & Row, 1967), 37 (see 15–36 on eschatology). Norman Perrin puts it simply, "Jesus proclaimed the eschatological Kingdom of God. . . ." *Rediscovering the Teaching of Jesus* (New York: Harper & Row, 1967), 56–57; see also *The Kingdom of God in the Teaching of Jesus* (Philadelphia: Westminster Press, 1963), 160–68. Along the same line: Amos N. Wilder, *Eschatology and Ethics in the Teachings of Jesus,* rev. ed. (New York: Harper & Row, 1950); Carl E. Braaten, *Eschatology and Ethics: Essays on the Theology and Ethics of the Kingdom of God* (Minneapolis: Augsburg Publishing House, 1974).

3. Although there is general scholarly agreement that "kingdom of God"

is an eschatological expression having to do with the ending of the world, there have been three major interpretations in the last hundred years. The first, initiated by Johannes Weiss and developed by Albert Schweitzer, *The Quest of the Historical Jesus: A Critical Study of Its Progress from Reimarus to Wrede* (New York: Macmillan Co., 1961), is called *consequent eschatology*: Jesus taught that the kingdom of God would arrive soon after his death in the imminent end of the world (and in this, they say, Jesus was mistaken). The second, initially proposed by C. H. Dodd, *The Parables of the Kingdom*, rev. ed. (New York: Charles Scribner's Sons, 1961), maintains that the kingdom has already arrived in the words and deeds of Jesus, and it is called *realized eschatology*. A third, mediating interpretation is associated with Joachim Jeremias, *The Parables of Jesus*, rev. ed. S. H. Hooke (New York: Charles Scribner's Sons, 1963), who suggests the expression "eschatology in process of realization." This might be called *progressive eschatology* (Crossan). Finally, others like J. D. Crossan, *In Parables: The Challenge of the Historical Jesus* (New York: Harper & Row, 1973), who want to get out of the "linear concept of time," suggest a *permanent eschatology*, the concept that the kingdom is always challenging our worlds and shattering our complacencies. Bultmann's existentialist interpretation of the eschatological now and Amos N. Wilder, Norman Perrin, and others who interpret the parables in contemporary categories of symbolism seem to follow this course.

4. Norman Perrin, after long years working with these issues is positive on two counts: (1) "That the Kingdom of God as a future expectation in the teaching of Jesus is not a matter of dispute in the current discussion," and (2) "no part of the teaching of Jesus is more difficult to reconstruct and interpret than that relating to the future." *Rediscovering*, 159–60, 154. He himself makes a valuable contribution with his study of parables, sayings, and actions of Jesus in his section on "Jesus and the Future" (154–206). Cf. also *Kingdom*, 190–99. An author who has reinstated and expanded once and again a futuristic interpretation of the teachings of Jesus is Richard H. Hiers, *The Kingdom of God in the Synoptic Tradition* (Gainesville: University Presses of Florida, 1970); *The Historical Jesus and the Kingdom of God: Present and Future in the Message of Jesus* (Gainesville: University Presses of Florida, 1973); *Jesus and the Future* (Atlanta: John Knox Press, 1981). W. G. Kümmel, after careful exegesis of all the relevant passages and constant dialogue with current scholarship, reaches the conclusion that "all these texts confirm that Jesus did indeed count on a shorter or longer period between his death and the parousia, but that he equally certainly proclaimed the threatening approach of the Kingdom of God within his generation." *Promise and Fulfillment: The Eschatological Message of Jesus*, trans. Dorothea M. Barton (New York: Oxford University Press, 1957), 87; see the whole chapter on "The Imminent Future of the Kingdom of God," 19–87.

5. R. Bultmann, *Jesus and the Word* (New York: Charles Scribner's Sons, 1958), 51, 158–59.

6. The parousia is painted with the bright colors of the popular celebrations in the big cities on occasion of the "coming" of the emperor. This final event is often referred to as "the second coming," but it is interesting to note that this common expression is not in the New Testament. "Parousia is 'advent arrival,' not 'second coming,'" says Bultmann, who reminds us that the latter was first used by Justin in the second century. *Theology of the New Testament* (New York: Charles Scribner's Sons, 1951), 1: 31. Cf. also J. Jeremias, *New Testament Theology* (New York: Charles Scribner's Sons, 1971), 273.

7. C. H. Dodd regards these as "crisis" parables which were originally intended by Jesus "to enforce his appeal to men to recognize that the Kingdom of God was present in all its momentous consequences," but later on were adapted by the early church for the waiting period between the resurrection and Jesus' coming in glory (*Parables of the Kingdom*, 122–39). Jeremias recognizes that there was "a shift of emphasis," to fill the needs of the church facing the delay of the parousia, though "its eschatological character was preserved." *Parables of Jesus*, 48–66. Kümmel, however, denies that the parables have been modified by the delay of the parousia and affirms, on the contrary, that they are really "parousia parables" from Jesus himself "intended to urge preparedness for the day of the appearance of the parousia which may occur at any time." He adds: "The parables lose all real meaning if the wakefulness for the unexpected coming of the Lord is interpreted as readiness for the judgment which is always in process. . . ." *Promise and Fulfillment*, 54–59.

8. Alfred C. Krass, *Five Lanterns at Sundown: Evangelism in a Chastened Mood* (Grand Rapids: Wm. B. Eerdmans, 1980), 64, 107, 177, 183.

9. There is also another simpler version in the noncanonical *Gospel of Thomas*, 64. See English version and commentary in John Dominic Crossan, *The Dark Interval: Towards a Theology of Story* (Allen, Tex.: Argus Communications), 108–19. Joachim Jeremias, *The Eucharistic Words of Jesus* (Philadelphia: Fortress Press, 1966), comments especially on Luke's text.

10. See Perrin, *Rediscovering*, 106–8.

11. This is the end of Kümmel's argument in his little book with precisely that title—*Promise and Fulfillment:* "In Jesus the kingdom of God came into being and in him it will be consummated. . . . Promise and fulfillment are therefore inseparably united for Jesus and depend on each other; for the promise is made sure by the fulfillment that has already taken place in Jesus . . . the inseparable union of hope and present experience demonstrate the fact that the true meaning of Jesus' eschatological message is to be found in its reference to God's action in Jesus himself . . . Jesus who would promise us the reign of God, because it was already being fulfilled in him" (p. 155).

On the eschatological meaning of the Last Supper, see Jeremias, *Eucharistic Words*, chaps. 4 and 5.

12. Krister Stendahl, "Your Kingdom Come: Notes for a Bible Study," in the Melbourne Conference volume *Your Kingdom Come* (Geneva: WCC, 1980), 76.

13. Ernst Lohmeyer, *Our Father: An Introduction to the Lord's Prayer* (New York: Harper & Row, 1965), 89ff. It has been widely acknowledged that the will of God and his kingdom were also related in the synagogue Kaddish prayer. It has been observed, however, that while the Kaddish speaks of the kingdom as "being established," the expression about its "coming" is typically from Jesus' language and perspective on the imminent kingdom (cf. N. Perrin, *Jesus and the Language of the Kingdom: Symbol and Metaphor in New Testament Interpretation* [Philadelphia: Fortress Press, 1980], 28; *Rediscovering*, 160; Joachim Jeremias, *The Lord's Prayer* [Philadelphia: Fortress Press, 1964], 22–23).

14. We need to remember that in Aramaic the original form of the Beatitudes would not have the verb "to be" either in present or past tenses, so its transliteration to Greek has to be judged by its context and by the structure of the saying itself.

15. "To enter the Kingdom refers to the future eschatological fulfillment of God's reign," concludes Aloysius M. Ambrozic, in his critical study of Mark 10:14–15, *The Hidden Kingdom: A Redactional-Critical Study of the References to the Kingdom of God in Mark's Gospel*, The Catholic Biblical Quarterly—Monograph Series, No. 2 (Washington, D.C.: Catholic Biblical Association of America, 1972), 139–43.

16. Hans Conzelmann, *Jesus* (Philadelphia: Fortress Press, 1973), 43–46. See also Oscar Cullmann, *Christology of the New Testament* (Philadelphia: Westminster Press, 1963) for an exhaustive treatment of the "Son of man" concept. Perrin provides an interpretation of the "Son of man" sayings by the early church in *Rediscovering*, 164–85. For Jeremias's point of view, see *New Testament Theology*, 257–76.

17. C. J. Cadoux quotes Weinel's seven differences between Jesus and the apocalypticists: (1) he did not write pseudonymously; (2) he spoke comfort as well as doom; (3) his pictures of the future were comparably simple; (4) eschatology was subordinate to the prophetic element; (5) he construed no numerical calculation as to the time of the end; (6) he was free from Jewish particularism; (7) he preached a present as well as a future kingdom. *The Historical Mission of Jesus* (New York: Harper & Brothers, 1943). For a different point of view, see Hiers, *Jesus and the Future*, especially chaps. 1, 6, and 7. "Jesus' proclamation of the Kingdom of God . . . indicates that his understanding of history was consistently eschatological, indeed, apocalyptic" (p. 87).

18. Georgia Harkness has an interesting and balanced discussion on the prophetic and apocalyptic elements of the kingdom in *Understanding the*

Kingdom of God (Nashville: Abingdon Press, 1974), 50–81. She proposes a composite picture of the kingdom, amalgamating the particular emphasis of each one of the current eschatologies: "There are points of truth and value in each one of the four types of eschatology. The *apocalyptic* stresses a sense of urgency and of God's power; the *prophetic* calls us to be active participants in the Kingdom process; the *realized* type reminds us of the Kingdom immediacy; the call to *existential* decision again emphasizes urgency but without biblical literalism. There is truth in each of these thrusts if they can be amalgamated" (p. 50). "Both the prophetic and the apocalyptic elements were absorbed into the mind and heart of Jesus" (p. 56). Jürgen Moltmann has made an illuminating analysis of the contrast between the "prophetic eschatology" and the "apocalyptic eschatology" in *Theology of Hope*, 124–38.

19. For a complete inventory of Jesus' futuristic sayings and his use of apocalyptic terminology, see Cadoux, *The Historic Mission of Jesus*.

20. Kümmel has summarized the point tersely: "Jesus' sayings about the future must not be understood as apocalyptic information, but as eschatological promise." *Promise and Fulfillment*, 155.

21. G. R. Beasley-Murray wrote a complete history of this theory in *Jesus and the Future: An Examination of the Criticism of the Eschatological Discourse, Mark 13, with Special Reference to the Little Apocalypse Theory* (London: Macmillan & Co., 1954), 1–171. See also Kümmel, *Promise and Fulfillment*, 95–104 and bibliographical references. Cf. Agustin del Agua Perez on Luke 21:5–36 in *Estudios Biblicos* 39 (1981): 285–313.

22. Cf. Beasley-Murray, *Jesus and the Future*, and Ambrozic's conclusions of his critical study, *The Hidden Kingdom*, 203–43. There is a growing trend among scholars to interpret the apocalyptic discourse as a Christian midrash, actualizing and applying Jesus' words and relating them to Old Testament texts to address the need of the Christian community after the destruction of the Temple in Jerusalem. See Agua Perez, *Estudios Biblicos* 39, text and bibliography, 286ff.

23. See Ambrozic's discussions in *The Hidden Kingdom* on "this generation" and "with power and glory," in his study of Mark 9:1 and 13:30.

24. The practical (paraenetic) intention of Mark 13 and parallels becomes crystal clear at the very end (13:33, 35–36), spelling out the message of the key verse (13:32). Ambrozic reaches the heart of Jesus' lapidary words on apocalyptic knowledge of the future and their meaning for evangelization today when he says: "The meaning of v. 32 can hardly be missed: Mark asserts that Jesus himself did not know the precise moment of the parousia. The primary purpose of the assertion lies, of course, in the parenesis which follows; since Jesus did not know, Christians do not know, and any attempt to calculate that moment is an impermissible and sinful prying into the secrets which are God's alone. Though Mark is convinced that there is a connection between the destruction of the Temple and the end (vv. 1–4),

and though this destruction is a sign of the nearness of the end (v. 29), he clearly separates the historical, and for him past, event from the future coming of the Son of Man. He insists that it must not be abused for the purpose of laying hands on what God has reserved for himself. Instead of being a reckoning device, the destruction of the Temple is made to serve ethical exhortation. Mark thus counteracts apocalyptic propaganda based on the illusion that with the fall of Jerusalem the end has arrived. 'The end is not yet.' . . ." *The Hidden Kingdom*, 230.

25. Actually, apocalyptic literature was born in times of repression and persecution of the faithful, and the original intention of these clandestine messages in apocalyptic key was to console the defenseless people of God and to keep up the faith of the saints before the overwhelming powers of this world. See Carlos Mesters, "A Coragem da Fe: Uma leitura de Historia a pastir dos aprimidos," in *Presenga e Tempo* (1979): 32–35.

26. Hans Küng, *On Being a Christian*, trans. Edward Quinn (New York: Doubleday & Co., 1969), 215.

27. Harkness, *Understanding the Kingdom*, 55.

28. Küng, *On Being a Christian*, 223.

Chapter 4

1. See chap. 1, n. 14 for bibliographical references for a study of the terms "kingdom" or "reign."

2. Practically all the sources we have quoted would insist on the dynamic character of the kingdom as proclaimed by Jesus. For instance, George Eldon Ladd says, "The key to Jesus' proclamation of the Kingdom of God is found in the dynamic understanding of that term"—"the inbreaking of God into the human history to establish his will." *Jesus and the Kingdom: The Eschatology of Biblical Realism* (New York: Harper & Row, 1964), 182ff. Norman Perrin says, "so far as the actual meaning of the expression translated Kingdom of God (Hebrew: *malkuth shamayim* and its cognates and their Aramaic equivalents) is concerned there is no doubt but that the primary and essential reference is to the sovereignty of God conceived of in the most concrete possible manner, i.e. to his *activity* in ruling." *Rediscovering the Teaching of Jesus* (New York: Harper & Row, 1967), 55. R. Schnackenburg puts it categorically: "the Kingdom of God is characterized not by latent authority but by the exercise of power, not by an office but a function. It is not a title but a deed." *God's Rule and Kingdom*, trans. John Murray (New York: Herder & Herder, 1963), 13. After quoting Schnackenburg, Perrin sharpens his definition: "The Kingdom of God is the power of God expressed in deeds; it is that which God does wherein it becomes evident that he is king. It is not a place or community ruled by God, it is not even the abstract idea of reign or kingship of God. It is quite concretely the activity of God as king." *Rediscovering*, 55.

3. Günther Bornkamm, in spite of his scholarly caution about the sources, reflects, in his brief summaries, this confrontational atmosphere of

Jesus' journey to Jerusalem: "This decision to go to Jerusalem is undoubtedly the turning-point in Jesus' life. . . . The reason why Jesus sets out with
his disciples on his journey to Jerusalem cannot be doubted. It was to
deliver the message of the coming Kingdom of God in Jerusalem also,
Jerusalem which Jesus himself calls the city of God, 'the city of the Great
King' (Matt. 5:35). . . . That the road to Jerusalem had to lead to new and
serious conflicts with the spiritual and temporal rulers, and that Jesus had to
reckon with the possibility of his own violent death, we have no reason to
doubt. . . . The sources do not tell us clearly at what moment his readiness
to accept death—a readiness which Jesus, as we know, demanded from his
disciples too—turned into the certainty of his imminent end. We may,
however, assume that first and foremost his journey to Jerusalem was
undertaken in order *to confront the people there, in the holy city, with the
message of the kingdom of God,* and to summon them at the eleventh hour
to make a decision." *Jesus of Nazareth,* trans. Irene McLuskey and Fraser
McLuskey with James M. Robinson (New York: Harper & Row, 1960), 154–
55, italics added.

   4. Jacques Ellul puts it in this way: "We are not marching toward the
Kingdom of God, but the Kingdom of God is bursting violently into our
times, into our milieu. It is breaking up the balanced order of march, the
timetables, and the organizations. It is alive in our midst. . . . This has been
the focal point of all my biblical and political interpretations, and it is now
being more confirmed by theologians and exegetes, who demonstrate that
the theological concepts of the New Testament are centered on the preaching of the Kingdom which is to come and which is coming." *Hope in a Time
of Abandonment* (New York: Seabury Press, 1973), 172.

   5. Jürgen Moltmann's definition of the kingdom includes this element of
contradiction and resistance: "The eschatological fulfilment of the liberating
lordship of God in history is termed the kingdom of God. The Greek word
basileia can mean both the actual rule of God in the world, and the
universal goal of that divine rule. . . . In history God rules through the word
of promise and the Spirit of freedom. Both are assailed and come up against
contradiction, resistance and antagonism. In history, therefore, God rules in
a disputed and hidden way." *The Church in the Power of the Spirit* (New
York: Harper & Row, 1977), 190.

   6. Perrin, *Rediscovering,* defends the authenticity of the saying over
against R. Bultmann and concludes that "this saying confirms what we have
learned already from other sayings, namely, that the time of God's activity
as king is now, and that the form of this activity can be envisaged in terms of
conflict. . . . The outcome of the battle may be sure, but the casualties are
going to be real, not sham" (p. 77). Ernst Käsemann considers it a most
enlightening passage, belonging to a very primitive tradition in which Jesus
ascribes John the Baptist with the unique eschatological role of ushering in
"the turning-point of the aeons." Actually, Käsemann uses this passage to

make one of the most definite christological affirmations in his study on "The Problem of the Historical Jesus." He asks: "But who then is this, who does justice to the Baptist and yet claims for himself a mission higher than that entrusted to John?" And he answers: "Evidently, he who brings with his Gospel the kingdom itself; a kingdom which can yet be obstructed and snatched away, for the very reason that it appears in the defenseless form of the Gospel." *Essays on New Testament Themes*, trans. W. J. Montague (Philadelphia: Fortress Press, 1982), 43.

7. W. G. Kümmel, after considering the different proposals, concludes: "No argument can be brought forward to tip the scale between these two exegeses, nor can either be definitely refuted; so the question must be left open." *Promise and Fulfillment: The Eschatological Message of Jesus*, trans. Dorothea M. Barton (New York: Oxford University Press, 1957), 123; see nn. 67 and 68 or references from interpreters on both sides. For the intriguing suggestion that the "violent men" may be another designation for the followers of Jesus (equivalent to "the poor," "the little ones," "the sinners"), see J. Jeremias, *New Testament Theology* (New York: Charles Scribner's Sons, 1971), 111–12.

8. Werner H. Kelber, *Mark's Story of Jesus* (Philadelphia: Fortress Press, 1979), 24–25.

9. Jacques Ellul's works are a good example of confrontational evangelization and an in-depth critique of present technological civilization from the perspective of the kingdom that is coming, challenging and transforming all our works and our old orders. Besides his early seminal work, *The Presence of the Kingdom* (New York: Seabury Press, 1967), published in French in 1948, the following are some of the better-known English translations of his many books: *The Technological Society* (New York: Random House, 1964); *The Meaning of the City* (Grand Rapids: Wm. B. Eerdmans, 1970); *The New Demons* (New York: Seabury Press, 1975); *The Ethics of Freedom* (Grand Rapids: Wm. B. Eerdmans, 1976).

10. See *metanoia, strepho,* and *epistrephein* in *TDNT* 4: 975–80; 7: 714–29. For a recent review and treatment of the subject, see Jim Wallis, *The Call to Conversion: Recovering the Gospel for These Times* (New York: Harper & Row, 1981), chap. 1 and bibliographical references.

11. Jon Sobrino, *Christology at the Crossroads: A Latin American Approach* (Maryknoll, N.Y.: Orbis Books, 1978), 50–51.

12. Ibid.

13. Gabriel Fackre develops this idea in *Word and Deed: Theological Themes in Evangelism* (Grand Rapids: Wm. B. Eerdmans, 1975).

14. Paul Loffler, "Conversion in the Bible," *Mission Trends No. 2: Evangelization,* ed. Gerald H. Anderson and Thomas F. Stransky (New York: Paulist Press; Grand Rapids: Wm. B. Eerdmans, 1975). For a challenging concept of conversion to Christ in the neighbor, see Gustavo Gutiérrez, *A Theology of Liberation* (Maryknoll, N.Y.: Orbis Books, 1973), 204–5.

15. Jim Wallis, *Sojourners* (September 1981): 16–17.

16. William R. Farmer in his challenging book, *Jesus and the Gospel* (Philadelphia: Fortress Press, 1982), reconstructs Jesus' public career from the death of John the Baptist to his own death in Jerusalem and points to the double and compound crisis (internal and external) that occurred during that brief span of time. "Central to this crisis was the opposition to Jesus by the religious authorities" (p. 25). "He struck at an important root of the problem—the self-righteousness of a scrupulous religious establishment" (p. 40). Farmer believes that "in this period of opposition by religious authorities responsible for upholding the law in the towns and cities outside Jerusalem, Jesus formulated his woes against the scribes and Pharisees. These utterances are uncompromising" (p. 42). The outcome of this confrontation was obvious: "Uncompromising words like these sealed the fate of Jesus. By their use he unmasked what many in positions of privilege and power could not bear to have unmasked. Jesus penetrated the facade of goodness behind which persons hid their lust for power. . . . After invective like this, the legal authorities were beside themselves to find some charge on which to get rid of Jesus" (p. 42).

17. Some years ago S. G. F. Brandon stirred up the waters with his work *Jesus and the Zealots* (New York: Charles Scribner's Sons, 1967) by pointing to the coincidences and relationships between the movement of Jesus and the Zealot movement; the former reached a crucial point with the dramatic incident of the "cleansing of the temple." For a different interpretation, see O. Cullmann, *Jesus and the Revolutionaries* (New York: Harper & Row, 1970).

18. William R. Farmer, *Jesus and the Gospel*, points also to the concomitancies of the scribal system with the political, economic, and religious establishment in Jerusalem that finally issued in an unholy alliance to destroy Jesus and his message: "The compliance of high priestly circles and the rest of the Jerusalem oligarchy was assured once Jesus made it clear that he called for changes not only in men's hearts, but in the institutions of Zion—specifically within the central institution, the Temple itself (Matt. 21:12–13). With the Pharisees, the high priests, and the elders of the people in concert, the Roman authorities, had they insisted on due process, would have risked a tear in the delicately woven fabric of political collaboration" (p. 42). "Ostensibly, in the interest of maintaining Jewish law and Roman order, Jesus was executed. . . . While Jesus died a righteous man by the standards of the Kingdom of Heaven, he did not go to his cross innocent of breaking the law as it was represented by the mores of the local populace. Nor was he innocent of disturbing the peace as it was preserved in and through imperial order. He was crucified in the end by the Romans as a political criminal" (p. 43).

19. Sobrino, *Christology*, 52.

20. Leonardo Boff, *Jesus the Liberator* (Maryknoll, N.Y.: Orbis Books, 1980).

21. A classic study of Jesus' sayings on the Suffering Servant is the one by Vincent Taylor, *Jesus and His Sacrifice: A Study of the Passion Sayings in the Gospels* (New York: Macmillan Co., 1955).

Chapter 5

1. Alfred Loisy, *The Gospel and the Church* (Philadelphia: Fortress Press, 1976), 166.

2. R. Bultmann, *New Testament Theology*, 2 vols., trans. Kendrick Grobel (New York: Charles Scribner's Sons, 1951, 1955).

3. See Werner Foerster and Gottfried Quell, "Lord," in *Bible Key Words*, vol. 8 (New York: Harper & Row, 1958).

4. W. G. Kümmel, *The Theology of the New Testament* (Nashville: Abingdon Press, 1973), 111–14.

5. C. H. Dodd, *The Apostolic Preaching and Its Developments* (New York: Harper & Row, 1964). See also Martin Dibelius, *From Tradition to Gospel* (New York: Attic Books, 1971); Archibald M. Hunter, *The Message of the New Testament* (Philadelphia: Westminster Press, 1944); Hans Werner Bartsch, ed., *Kerygma and Myth: A Theological Debate* (New York: Harper & Row, 1961).

6. See the concept of *paradosis* in New Testament dictionaries. Cf. Archibald M. Hunter, *Paul and His Predecessors* (Philadelphia: Westminster Press, 1964).

7. W. D. Davies, *Invitation to the New Testament* (Garden City, N.Y.: Doubleday & Co., 1966), 50–62.

8. Leslie Newbigin, *The Open Secret* (London: SPCK, 1978), 44.

9. John Bright, *The Kingdom of God* (Nashville: Abingdon Press, 1953), 215–16.

10. O. E. Evans, "The Kingdom of God," *Interpreter's Dictionary of the Bible* (Nashville: Abingdon Press, 1962), 3: 24.

11. Agustin del Agua Perez, "El Cumplimento del Reino de Dios en la Mision de Jesus," *Estudios Biblicos* 38 (1979–80): 292.

12. J. D. Crossan, *The Dark Interval: Towards a Theology of Story* (Niles, Ill.: Argus Communications, 1975), 124–26.

13. Jürgen Moltmann, *The Crucified God* (New York: Harper & Row, 1974).

14. Jürgen Moltmann, *Theology of Hope* (New York: Harper & Row, 1967), 218–24.

15. W. G. Kümmel, *Theology*, 322–33.

16. Evans, "Kingdom of God."

17. Cf. Hunter, *Paul and His Predecessors*, 10–13. Herman N. Ridderbos, *Paul and Jesus* (Phillipsburg, N.J.: Presbyterian and Reformed Publishing Co., 1958).

18. Michael Green, *Evangelism in the Early Church* (Grand Rapids: Wm. B. Eerdmans, 1975), 51.

19. Cf. Archibald M. Hunter, *The Gospel According to St. Paul* (Philadelphia: Westminster Press, 1967). I had just finished this chapter when I came across two recent articles on this subject reaching very coincidental conclusions: J. Andrew Kirk, "en Torno al concepto del reino en Pablo," *Revista Biblica* (1979): 171–72, and Irene W. de Foulkes, "El Reino de Dios y Pablo," *Vida y Pensamiento* (July–December 1982): 9–24.

20. John Knox, *Chapters in a Life of Paul* (Nashville: Abingdon Press, 1950), 128, 138–41, 158, and L. Cerfaux, *Christ in the Theology of St. Paul* (New York: Herder & Herder, 1959).

21. M. Arias, *Venga tu Reino* (Mexico: Casa Unida de Publicaciones, 1980), 37–53.

22. See Rosemary Ruether, *The Radical Kingdom: The Western Experience of Messianic Hope* (New York: Paulist Press, 1970). It is interesting to see that Albert Schweitzer was already pointing to the eclipse of the kingdom in the whole history of Christianity: "What Paul firmly grasped was later lost hold of (the inner connection between the conception of redemption through Christ and a living belief in the Kingdom of God). When Christianity became hellenized there grew up a conception of redemption through Christ which no longer stood within that of the Kingdom but alongside it . . . and thus it has continued through the centuries. . . . In Catholicism and in the Protestantism of the Reformers, both of which had their structures determined by the form which Christianity has taken in the process of being hellenized, Christian doctrine is dominated by the idea of redemption based upon the atoning death of Jesus for the forgiveness of sins, alongside of which the belief in the Kingdom of God maintains a not too vigorous existence." *The Mysticism of Paul the Apostle*, 2d ed. (London: A. & C. Black, 1953). For Protestant understandings of the kingdom, see W. A. Visser't Hooft, *The Kingship of Christ* (New York: Harper & Brothers, 1948); H. Richard Niebuhr, *The Kingdom of God in America* (New York: Harper & Brothers, 1959).

Chapter 6

1. Gabriel Fackre, *Do and Tell: Engagement Evangelism in the Seventies* (Grand Rapids: Wm. B. Eerdmans, 1973).

2. G. R. Beasley-Murray, *Preaching the Gospel from the Gospels*, rev. ed. (London: Epworth Press, 1965).

3. Ibid.

4. Gabriel Fackre, *The Christian Story* (Grand Rapids: Wm. B. Eerdmans, 1978), 12.

5. *Your Kingdom Come* (Geneva: WCC, 1980), 93.

6. Cf. Donald G. Bloesch, *Essentials of Evangelical Theology* (New York: Harper & Row, 1978), 1: 7–23. John D. Woodbridge, ed., *The Evangelicals:*

What They Believe, Who They Are, How They Are Changing (Nashville: Abingdon Press, 1975).

7. Juan Luis Segundo, *The Hidden Motives of Pastoral Action* (Maryknoll, N.Y.: Orbis Books, 1972), 113.

8. *Your Kingdom Come*, 76.

9. Albert C. Outler, *Evangelism in the Wesleyan Spirit* (Nashville: Discipleship Resources, n.d.).

10. Henri J. Nouwen, *The Wounded Healer: Ministry in Contemporary Society* (Garden City, N.Y.: Doubleday & Co., 1972), 32–33.

11. Paul Tillich, *The Shaking of Foundations* (New York: Charles Scribner's Sons, 1948), 162.

12. Documents for the WCC assembly on "Jesus Christ the Life of the World."

13. *Your Kingdom Come*, 199.

14. Ibid., 200.

15. Ibid., 164–65.

16. Ibid., 86.

17. J. Jeremias, *The Eucharistic Words of Jesus* (Philadelphia: Fortress Press, 1966), 41ff.

18. *Your Kingdom Come*, 203–7. Ian Bria, "Eucharist and Evangelism," in *Monthly Letter About Evangelism* (Geneva: WCC, March–April 1981). Jeremias has reconstructed in a powerful way the original atmosphere of the Last Supper and its central meaning as Jesus' final donation of himself and the assurance of the gift of forgiveness as anticipation of the kingdom. See *Eucharistic Words of Jesus*, chap. 5.

19. M. Arias, "Centripetal Mission on Hospitality Evangelization," *Missiology* (January 1982).

20. Kosuke Koyama, "The Crucified Christ Challenges Human Power," *Your Kingdom Come* (Geneva: WCC, 1980), 162, 166.

21. Section II Report, "The Kingdom of God and Human Struggles," in *Your Kingdom Come*, 180.

Chapter 7

1. Hendrikus Berkhof, *Christ, the Meaning of History* (Richmond: John Knox Press, 1966), 204.

2. Robert C. Aldridge, "After Nuclear Holocaust, Business As Usual," *Los Angeles Times*, 15 February 1981, V, 5. John Bennett, "Countering the Theory of Limited Nuclear War," *The Christian Century* (January 7–14, 1981): 10–13.

3. "The Last Epidemic," movie by the Physicists Association of San Francisco and the ABC movie "The Day After." There is also an abundant literature on the nuclear threat. A very helpful review on "Nuclear Issues Resources" was published in *The Christian Century* (September 14–21, 1983): 819–27; see also (September 28, 1983): 850–54.

4. Hans Küng, *On Being a Christian*, trans. Edward Quinn (New York: Doubleday & Co., 1976), 223.

5. W. A. Visser't Hooft, *The Kingship of Christ* (New York: Harper & Brothers, 1948), 83.

6. Ferdinand Hahn, *Mission in the New Testament* (Naperville, Ill.: Alec R. Allenson, 1965), 51. Oscar Cullmann, "Eschatology and Mission in the New Testament," in *The Background of the New Testament and Its Eschatology*, ed. W. D. Davies and D. Daube (New York: Cambridge University Press, 1956), 409–21. For a different point of view see John G. Gager, *Kingdom and Community: The Social World of Early Christianity* (Englewood Cliffs, N.J.: Prentice-Hall, 1975), 39.

7. Carl E. Braaten, *The Flaming Center: A Theology of Christian Mission* (Philadelphia: Fortress Press, 1977), 29–36, 42.

8. Jürgen Moltmann, *Theology of Hope* (New York: Harper & Row, 1967), 224–25.

9. Braaten, *Flaming Center*, 43.

10. Ibid., 54.

11. Wolfhart Pannenberg, *Theology and the Kingdom of God* (Philadelphia: Westminster Press, 1969), 53, 61.

12. Lenwood G. Davies, *I Have a Dream: The Life and Times of Martin Luther King, Jr.* (Westport, Conn.: Negro University Press, 1973), 263.

13. James H. Forest, "Astonishing Hope," *Sojourners* (February 1980): 19.

14. Rubem Alves, "Christian Realism, Ideology of the Establishment," *Christianity and Crisis* (September 17, 1973): 175ff.

15. Rosemary Ruether, *The Radical Kingdom: The Western Experience of Messianic Hope* (New York: Harper & Row, 1970).

16. Sergio Torres and John Eagleson, eds., *The Challenge of Basic Christian Communities* (Maryknoll, N.Y.: Orbis Books, 1980).

17. The Melbourne Conference dealt with mission and evangelism in relation to the powers in its Section IV on "Christ—Crucified and Risen—Challenges Human Power." In this context, prophetic evangelization is called forth: "There are many different situations in which the churches are called to challenge the powers. In some situations the powers are clearly oppressive; other situations are 'mixed,' that is to say, at some points the powers seem to be acting in ways which affirm the humanity of people; sometimes by the grace of God they embody higher levels of justice because of their responsiveness to the needs and rights of the citizens. The criterion for determining the relation to the powers is the extent to which God's creative, liberating, and serving power is evidenced in their actions, and the extent to which equality is established. . . . When the churches challenge the powers in the name of people who are being dehumanized, the credibility of the churches with the oppressed is put to test. . . . In such situations the churches must be prepared to be minorities, but they can be

creative minorities. . . . In a world of large-scale robbery and genocide, Christian evangelism can be honest and authentic only if it stands clearly against these injustices which are diametrically opposed to the kingdom of God." *Your Kingdom Come* (Geneva: WCC, 1980), 211, 218.

18. Billy Graham, "A Clarification," *Christianity Today* (January 1943): 416. Quoted by Richard Quebedeaux in *The Young Evangelicals* (New York: Harper & Row, 1974), 35.

19. D.I.A.L., Paris, 1978.

20. "A Martyr's Abiding Hope," *Sojourners* (May 14, 1980).

21. Placido Erdozain, *Archbishop Romero: Martyr of Salvador*, trans. John McFadden and Ruth Warner (Maryknoll, N.Y.: Orbis Books, 1981).

22. Martin Lange and Reinhold Iblacker, eds., *Witnesses of Hope: The Persecution of Christians in Latin America* (Maryknoll, N.Y.: Orbis Books, 1981).

23. *The Christian Century* (September 16, 1981): 898–902.

Chapter 8

1. Robert E. Coleman, *The Master Plan of Evangelism* (Westwood, N.J.: Fleming H. Revell, 1963).

2. Donald McGavran, *Understanding Church Growth* (Grand Rapids: Wm. B. Eerdmans, 1970). C. Peter Wagner, *Our Own Kind* (Atlanta: John Knox Press, 1979).

3. See "Response to Lausanne," in *Let the Earth Hear His Voice*, ed. J. D. Douglas, International Congress on World Evangelization (Minneapolis: World Wide Publications, 1975). C. René Padilla, ed., *The New Face of Evangelicalism* (Downers Grove, Ill.: Inter-Varsity Press, 1976).

4. Faith Annette Sand and William Cook, "Winds of Change in Latin America," *The Other Side* (April 1980): 14–23. See also articles in *Sojourners*, passim; *Occasional Bulletin of Missionary Research* (July 1980); *International Review of Mission* (July 1979); *Priests, USA* (February 1979); *Christianity and Crisis* (September 1981); *Missiology* (July 1980). Cf. Sergio Torres and John Eagleson, eds., *The Challenge of Basic Christian Communities* (Maryknoll, N.Y.: Orbis Books, 1980).

5. Waldron Scott, *Bring Forth Justice: A Contemporary Perspective on Mission* (Grand Rapids: Wm. B. Eerdmans, 1980), 165–66, 206, 211.

6. Ronald E. Osborn, from a lecture. See Alexander Campbell and others on "Our Name," *Millennial Harbinger* (November 1839; January 1840), 17–29, 402–3.

7. Eduard Schweizer, *The Good News According to St. Mark* (Atlanta: John Knox Press, 1977), 49.

8. Juan Stam, as quoted by Orlando Costas, *Integrity in Mission: The Inner Life and Outreach of the Church* (New York: Harper & Row, 1979).

9. Jim Wallis, *Sojourners* (September 1981): 18.

10. Scott, *Bring Forth Justice*, 174.

11. George Eldon Ladd, *Jesus and the Kingdom: The Eschatology of Biblical Realism* (New York: Harper & Row, 1964), 251.

12. Ibid.

13. Schweizer, *Good News According to St. Mark*, 386.

14. Dietrich Bonhoeffer, *The Cost of Discipleship* (New York: Macmillan Co., 1963), 50–51.

15. Werner H. Kelber, *The Kingdom in Mark: A New Place and a New Time* (Philadelphia: Fortress Press, 1974), 14.

16. Alvaro Barreiro, *Basic Ecclesial Communities: The Evangelization of the Poor* (Maryknoll, N.Y.: Orbis Books, 1982), 9.

17. *Latin America in the Light of the Council* (Washington, D.C.: National Conference of Catholic Bishops, 1968).

18. Esther Arias and Mortimer Arias, *The Cry of My People* (New York: Friendship Press, 1980), chap. 4.

19. Mortimer Arias, *Venga tu Reino: La Memoria Subversiva de Jesus* (Mexico City: Casa Unida de Publicaciones, 1980), 163–64.

20. Martin Lange and Reinhold Iblacker, eds., *Witnesses of Hope: The Persecution of Christians in Latin America* (Maryknoll, N.Y.: Orbis Books, 1981), 27–36.

21. Ibid.

22. Ibid.

23. Ibid.

24. Ibid.

25. Claude Geffre, *The Mystical and Political Dimension of the Christian Faith* (New York: Seabury Press, 1975), 57ff.; Gustavo Gutiérrez, *A Theology of Liberation* (Maryknoll, N.Y.: Orbis Books, 1973), 204–5.

End of the Eclipse?

1. "Astonishing Hope," *Sojourners* (February 1980): 17.

2. David O. Moberg, *The Great Reversal: Evangelism Versus Social Concern* (Philadelphia: A. J. Holman, 1977).

3. E. Stanley Jones, *The Unshakeable Kingdom and the Unchanging Person* (Nashville: Abingdon Press, 1972), 21.

4. *The Methodist Hymnal* (Nashville: Methodist Publishing House, 1966), No. 410.

Scripture Index

OLD TESTAMENT

Genesis
1—89

Psalms
81:16—29
93:1—14
97:1-6—14
126:6—28
145:13—14

Proverbs
29:18—90

Isaiah
2—90

9:3—28
22:13—85
25:6-9—24
26:19—22
29:9-10, 18-19—22
35:5-6, 8—22
40:9-10—15
41:27—15
42:18—22
43:8—22
52:7—15, 22
52:10—15
53—52
58:6—4

60:6—15
61:1-2—4, 15
61:1-3—22

Jeremiah
31:31—29

Joel
3:13—28

Micah
4—90

Zechariah
8:8, 19-23—29

NEW TESTAMENT

Matthew
2:5—20
2:10-11—20
3:1-8—20
3:12—28
4:6-8, 29—36
4:8-9—9
5:20—32
5:24—112
5:35—43
6:1-6—33
6:9-10—31
6:12—112
6:14-15—21, 112

7:9-11—17
7:13-14—44
7:16-19—47
7:21—32
8:11-12—32, 35
9:1—33
9:2—72
9:11-13—24
9:13—72
9:14-17—23
9:35—3
9:36—78
9:37-38—28
10—6

10:16—46, 108
10:22—33
10:23—33
10:24—109
10:31—33
10:34-36—43
10:40-42—33
11:3—22
11:5—17, 22
11:5-6—3
11:9—15
11:11—15

147

2:36—56, 69
2:36-38—114
2:38-39—72
2:41-47—62
2:47—105
3:1-10—75
3:1-26—62
3:12-26—57
4:1-37—62
4:8-12—57
4:11—61
5:15-16—75
5:27-32—62
5:40-42—62
6:7—62
7:59—56
8:5-7—75
8:12—59
9:2—103
9:33-34—75
10:34—114
10:34-43—57
10:36—70
10:37-39—59
10:38—69
11:26—102
14:8-11—75
14:22—59
19:8—59
19:9—103
19:11-12—75
19:23—103
22:4—103
24:14, 22—103
28:23—59, 60
28:30-31—60
28:31—59

Romans
1:1-5—57

1:14-16—62
2:16—62
10:9—56, 57
14:17—63
16:25—62

1 Corinthians
1:2—56
1:22-24—61
1:23—58
2:2—58
4:20—63
6:9—63
9:20—62
11:26—31, 81
15:1-11—57
15:3-4—58
15:24-26—64
15:28—64, 86
16:22—55, 56

2 Corinthians
4:3—62

Galatians
1:6ff.—62
5:19-21—63
6:7-9—28

Ephesians
1:10—86
2:20—61
5:5—63
6:12—117

Philippians
1:21-23—85
2:6-7—82
4:5—56

Colossians
1:13-14—63

1 Thessalonians
1:10—58
2:12—63

2 Thessalonians
1:5—63
1:7—58

2 Timothy
2:8—62

Hebrews
13:12—82

James
5:14—77

1 Peter
2:5-8—61
2:7—43
3:15—97

1 John
3:16—112
3:17-18—112
4:7-8, 20—112
4:10—112
4:19—112

Revelation
1:9—99
11:15—86
14:15, 18—28
21—89
22:20—55, 56, 99

Author Index

Subject Index

153